Papatango Theatre Company and Park Theatre present

**THE WORLD PREMIERE OF THE WINNER OF THE 2024 PAPATANGO NEW WRITING PRIZE**

# The Meat Kings! (Inc.) Of Brooklyn Heights

by Hannah Doran

*The Meat Kings! (Inc.) Of Brooklyn Heights* was first produced by Papatango Theatre Company and Park Theatre, London, from 30 October – 29 November 2025.

# The Meat Kings! (Inc.) Of Brooklyn Heights
by Hannah Doran

**Cast**
(in alphabetical order)

| | |
|---|---|
| Paula | **Jackie Clune** |
| JD | **Marcello Cruz** |
| Billy | **Ash Hunter** |
| T | **Mithra Malek** |
| David | **Eugene McCoy** |

**Creatives**

| | |
|---|---|
| Director | **George Turvey** |
| Set & Costume Designer | **Mona Camille** |
| Lighting Designer | **Bethany Gupwell** |
| Composer & Sound Designer | **Asaf Zohar** |
| Movement Director | **Rachael Nanyonjo** |
| Costume Supervisor | **Natalia Alvarez** |
| Dialect Coach | **Caitlin Stegemoller** |
| Assistant Director | **Hope Wishart** |
| Casting Director | **Nadine Rennie** CDG |
| Producer for Papatango | **Chris Foxon** |
| Producer for Park Theatre | **Joshua Goodman** |
| Production Manager | **Ian Taylor for eStage** |
| Stage Manager | **Reuben Bojang** |
| Assistant Stage Manager | **Mia Stubbings** |
| Assistant Stage Manager | **Kal Chapman** |
| Lighting Programmer & Production Electrician | **Matthew Carnazza** |

**Jackie Clune** | Paula

Theatre includes *Otherland* (Almeida Theatre); *Just For One Day* (Old Vic); *Grenfell* (National Theatre/ St Ann's Warehouse; New York); *Dr Semmelweis* (Bristol Old Vic); *Measure for Measure*; *[BLANK]* and *The Vote* (Donmar Warehouse); *Julius Caesar*; *Henry IV* and *The Tempest* (Donmar Warehouse/St Ann's Warehouse; New York); *Utility* (Orange Tree Theatre); *Candide* (Menier Chocolate Factory); *Fallen Angels* (Salisbury Playhouse); *9 to 5: The Musical* (UK tour); *Billy Elliot: The Musical* (West End); *Mamma Mia!* (international tour) and *Mogadishu* (Lyric Hammersmith).

Television includes *The Couple Next Door*, *Grace*, *Towards Zero*, *Mandy*, *Motherland*, *Borderline*, *Stephen*, *Three Girls*, *Ghosts*, *Father Brown*, *Marriage* and *The Blue*.

Film includes *The Great Escaper*, *Denial*, *Breathtaking* and *Jawbone*.

Jackie is also a stand-up comedian and the author of four books.

**Marcello Cruz** | JD

Marcello trained at Guildhall School of Music and Drama on the Josephine Hart Poetry Foundation Scholarship.

Theatre includes *Rare Earth Mettle* (Royal Court Theatre); *Sweat* (Royal Exchange Theatre); *Much Ado About Nothing* (Shakespeare's Globe); *Romeo and Juliet* (Orange Tree Theatre) and *Twelfth Night* and *Hamlet* (Shakespeare's Rose Theatre).

Television includes *Silo*, *Alex Rider* and *The Man Who Fell To Earth*.

Film includes *The 355*.

**Ash Hunter** | Billy

Theatre includes *Grenfell* (National Theatre/St Ann's Warehouse; New York); *Macbeth* (Leeds Playhouse); *Wuthering Heights* (National Theatre); *Hamilton* (West End); *HY Brasil* (Old Vic); *Pitcairn* (Shakespeare's Globe); *God's Property* (Soho Theatre); *Unrivalled Landscape* (Orange Tree Theatre); *A Midsummer Night's Dream* (Almeida Theatre); *Gravity* (Birmingham Rep) and *A Clockwork Orange* (Theatre Royal Stratford East).

Television includes *Grace*, *Alma's Not Normal*, *Bridgerton*, *Harlots*, *The Trial of Christine Keeler*, *Death in Paradise*, *The Secret Agent*, *Wolfblood*, *Switch* and *Maya*.

Film includes *Intrigo: Dear Agnes* and *The Thief*.

**Mithra Malek** | T

Theatre includes *Romeo + Juliet* (Circle in the Square Theatre, New York) and *Hamlet*, *The Cherry Orchard* and *Love From a Stranger* (Theatre Royal Windsor).

Television includes *Anatomy of a Scandal*.

Film includes *Hamlet*, *Party People*, *Tala* and *Now You See Me 2*.

**Eugene McCoy** | David

Theatre includes *Girl From the North Country*, *Groundhog Day* and *A Christmas Carol* (Old Vic); *Natasha, Pierre and the Great Comet of 1812* (Donmar Warehouse); *The 39 Steps* (Trafalgar Theatre/UK tour); *Legally Blonde* (Regent's Park Open Air Theatre); *The Man in the White Suit* (West End/Theatre Royal Bath); *Man of La Mancha* (London Coliseum); *The*

*Pajama Game* (West End/Chichester Festival Theatre); *American Psycho* (Almeida Theatre); *Little Shop of Horrors* (UK tour); *They're Playing Our Song (*Menier Chocolate Factory); *Oklahoma!* (Chichester Festival Theatre); *Jersey Boys*, *Guys and Dolls* and *Mamma Mia!* (West End) and *Hollywood Symphonic* (EC1 International).

Television includes *Donkey*, *Little Crackers* and *Unforgotten*.

Film includes *Wonka*, *Matilda* and *Paddington 2.*

**Hannah Doran** | Playwright

Hannah is a British-Irish playwright and screenwriter whose work has been developed and workshopped in the UK, USA and Australia. She received her MFA from NYU's Tisch School of the Arts in 2018. She was selected for the National MFA Playwrights' Festival in 2017 with her short play *A Last Night on Earth*, which was produced by Theater Masters in Aspen, Colorado, and subsequently Off-Off-Broadway at Theater for the New City. Based in London, Hannah is a bookseller and a member of the National Theatre's script reading team.

**George Turvey** | Director

George co-founded Papatango in 2007 and became sole Artistic Director in 2013. He has been awarded the Genesis Foundation Prize and named in *The Stage* 25.

He has dramaturged all of Papatango's productions, including the Olivier Award-winning *Old Bridge*. Theatre direction for Papatango includes: *The Watch House* and *The Silence and the Noise* (UK tours); *Some Demon* (Arcola Theatre/Bristol Old Vic, nominated for 4 OffWestEnd Awards including Best Director); *Shook* (Southwark Playhouse/UK tour, nominated for 7 OffWestEnd Awards including Best Director and Best Production; also broadcast on Sky Arts); *Here* (Southwark Playhouse); *Hanna* (Arcola Theatre/UK tour); *The Annihilation of Jessie Leadbeater* (ALRA); *After Independence* (Arcola Theatre/BBC Radio 4, winner of the Alfred Fagon Audience Award); *Leopoldville* (Tristan Bates Theatre) and *Angel* (Pleasance London/Tristan Bates Theatre).

Film direction for Papatango includes *Heathen Land*.

George trained as a director on the National Theatre Studio Directors' course and as an actor at the Academy of Live and Recorded Arts. He has appeared on stage and screen throughout the UK and internationally, including the lead roles in the world premiere of Arthur Miller's *No Villain* (Old Red Lion Theatre/West End) and *Batman Live* World Arena Tour. He is co-author of *Being A Playwright: A Career Guide For Writers*.

**Mona Camille** | Set & Costume Designer

Mona is an award-winning designer with a background in architecture. She works across theatre, dance and film in the UK and internationally.

Theatre includes *We Aren't Kids Anymore* (Savoy Theatre); *How To Fight Loneliness* (Park Theatre); *Kim's Convenience* (Riverside Studios/Park Theatre/UK tour); *More... Ghost Stories by Candlelight* (Sam Wanamaker Playhouse/UK tour); *We All Know How This Ends* (Theatre Royal Stratford East); *Canned Goods* (Southwark Playhouse) and *Milk & Gall* (Theatre503).

Screen work includes *Camaleonte* and *Loyal*.

Associate design includes *A View from the Bridge* (Headlong Theatre/Chichester Festival Theatre/Octagon Bolton/Rose Theatre); *Henry V* (Headlong Theatre/Sam Wanamaker Playhouse/UK tour); *Worth* (Arcola Theatre/Storyhouse Chester) and *Raya* (Hampstead Theatre).

Mona is also a tutor and lecturer at both the Architectural Association School of Architecture and Buckinghamshire New University.

**Bethany Gupwell** | Lighting Designer

Bethany trained at the Royal Central School of Speech and Drama. In 2018 she was awarded the Association of Lighting Designers' Francis Reid Award.

Theatre includes *All's Well That Ends Well* (Shakespeare's Globe); *Larmes de Couteat / Full Moon in March* (Royal Opera House); *Escaped Alone / What If Only* and *Shed: Exploded View* (Royal Exchange Theatre); *Twelfth Night*, *Quiet Songs*, *A Play for the Living in a Time of Extinction* and *Lay Down Your Burdens* (Barbican); *La Voix Humaine*

(Opéra National du Rhin); *Dead Woman* (Schaubuhne); *Visit from an Unknown Woman*, *This Much I Know*, *To Have and to Hold* (OffWestEnd Award nomination), *Little Scratch* and *Wolf Cub* (Hampstead Theatre); *The Earthworks* (Young Vic); *Robin Hood* (Theatre Royal Bath); *Here* and *The Woods* (Southwark Playhouse); *Lady Dealer* (Bush Theatre); *War & Culture*, *Little Scratch* and *Keep Watching* (New Diorama Theatre); *Ignition* (Frantic Assembly); *The Pirate, the Princess and the Platypus* (Polka Theatre); *A-Typical Rainbow* (OffWestEnd Award nomination, Turbine Theatre); *In Praise Of Love*, *Rice* and *Little Baby Jesus* (Orange Tree Theatre); *Little Brother*, *Brown Girls Do It Too: Mama Told Me Not to Come*, *Fitter* and *Wonder Winterland* (Soho Theatre) and *Talking Heads* (Watford Palace Theatre).

**Asaf Zohar** | Composer & Sound Designer

Asaf trained at the Royal College of Music.

Theatre includes *Ballet Shoes* and *The Estate* (National Theatre); *Measure for Measure* (RSC); *Macbeth* (UK & international tours); *God of Carnage* (Lyric Hammersmith); *Some Demon*, *Here* and *The Silence and the Noise* (Papatango); *Sessions* and *Whitewash* (Soho Theatre); *Peter Pan Reimagined* (Birmingham Rep); *Farewell Mister Haffman*, *The Shape of Things* and *Disruption* (Park Theatre); *My Mother's Funeral: The Show* (UK tour); *Dennis of Penge* (Guildhall School of Music and Drama/Ovalhouse/Albany Deptford); *Sorry, You're Not A Winner* (Bristol Old Vic/Theatre Royal, Plymouth); *Nanny* (Bristol Old Vic); *Captain Amazing*, *The Bleeding Tree*, *The Bit-Players* and *Romeo and Juliet* (Southwark Playhouse); *Waiting for Anya* (Barn Theatre); *Bright Half Life* (King's Head Theatre); *Wild Country* (Camden People's Theatre); *The Goose Who Flew* (Half Moon Theatre) and *The Shadowpunk Revolutions* (Edinburgh Festival).

Television includes *Reggie Yates: Extreme Russia*; *Reggie Yates: Race Riots USA*; *Reggie Yates: Extreme UK*; *Reggie Yates: Extreme South Africa* and *Dispatches: Taliban Child Fighters*, in addition to in-house work for Virgin Media and various media companies.

His film work has been shown at Cannes, BAFTA, Edinburgh and Encounters festivals.

**Rachael Nanyonjo** | Movement Director

Rachael is a Ugandan-British director, choreographer and movement director. She trained at Middlesex University and Roehampton University.

Theatre as movement director includes *Macbeth* (ETT/Lyric Hammersmith); *My Mother's Funeral* (Edinburgh Festival/Bristol Old Vic/Coventry Belgrade/Soho Playhouse, New York); *Stolen Ground* (Théâtre des Capucins, Luxembourg); *Moby Dick* (UK tour); *Boys From the Blackstuff* (Liverpool Royal Court/National Theatre/West End); *Misty* (West End/The Shed, New York); *The P Word* (Olivier Award Winner, Bush Theatre); *Dumbledore Is So Gay* (Southwark Playhouse); *The Tempest* (Shakespeare's Globe); *Purple Snowflakes & Titty Wanks* (Abbey Theatre/Royal Court Theatre); *Trouble in Mind* (National Theatre); *Changing Destiny* (Young Vic); *Either* (Hampstead Theatre); *Two Trains Running* (ETT/Royal & Derngate Theatres); *Sleeping Beauty* (Theatre Royal Stratford East); *Shebeen* (Nottingham Playhouse/Theatre Royal Stratford East) and *Bernstein's MASS* (Southbank Centre).

Theatre as director includes *Recognition* (Talawa Theatre, OffWestEnd Award-nominated for Best Director and Best Choreography and winner of the OffWestEnd Award for Best Musical Direction) and *Next Please* (Almeida Theatre).

Theatre as associate director includes *Retrograde* (West End), *Play On* (Talawa Theatre) and *Newsies* (Troubadour Theatre).

Television includes *A Pack of Lies*, *CBEEBIES: Christmas in Storyland* and *Pirates*.

Film includes *Love At First Sight*.


**Natalia Alvarez** | Costume Supervisor

Natalia trained at Wimbledon College of Arts.

Theatre as costume supervisor includes *Antony and Cleopatra* (Shakespeare's Globe); *Uncle Vanya*, *Duet for One*, *Arms and the Man* and *Statements After an Arrest Under the Immorality Act* (Orange Tree Theatre); *Journey of a Refugee* (Theatre Rites) and *Under the Kundè Tree* and *Here* (Southwark Playhouse).

Theatre as associate designer includes *Friends the Parody Musical* (UK tour); *Saturday Night Fever - Das Kult Musical* (German tour); *Nine* and *Assassins* (Royal College of Music); *Oscar at the Crown* (The Crown); *Midnight Cowboy* (Southwark Playhouse); *Nikita Kuzman: Midnight Dancer* (UK tour); *A Christmas Carol* (Lowry); *The Creakers Musical* (Theatre Royal, Plymouth); *Aladdin* (Everyman Theatre, Cheltenham); *Lizzie* (Hope Mill Theatre) and *I Am Here: Oti Mabuse* (UK tour).

Theatre as costume designer includes *No Limits* (Turbine Theatre); *Chess* (Leicester Curve); *Closer Than Ever* (Charing Cross Theatre); *Lift: The Musical* (Southwark Playhouse); *The Last Five Years* (Minack Theatre) and *Paperboy* (Lyric Theatre, Belfast).

### **Caitlin Stegemoller** | Dialect Coach

Caitlin is a London-based voice and dialect coach originally from the USA. Caitlin trained at the Royal Central School of Speech and Drama and the University of Arizona.

Theatre includes *Here We Are* and *The Witches* (National Theatre); *Operation Mincemeat* (Broadway/West End); *Fiddler on the Roof* (Regent's Park Open Air Theatre); *The Band's Visit* (Donmar Warehouse); *untitled f\*ck m\*ss s\*\*gon* (Royal Exchange/Young Vic); *The Code* (Southwark Playhouse); *Disruption* (Park Theatre); *Buyer & Cellar* (King's Head Theatre); *RIDE: A New Musical* (Leicester Curve) and *The Winter's Tale* (Minack Theatre).

Television includes *Silo*.

Radio includes *People Who Knew Me*.

Caitlin is a senior voice tutor at ArtsEd and a designated Linklater Voice teacher.

### **Hope Wishart** | Assistant Director

Hope trained at Drama Centre, Bristol University, Cine Studio Paris and LAMDA.

Theatre includes *A Microscopic Odyssey* (Mycelium Theatre Company at Theatre503); *The Oedipus Family Portrait* (Athens Conservatoire); *Julie: After Strindberg* (Alma Tavern); *All that Beauty* (Divaldo Archa, Prague); *Wall(s)*

(Tobacco Factory Theatres) and *Love and Information* (The Loco Club).

Film includes *Still a' Dancing*, *The Sound of Home*, *My Love, My Lebanon*, *Petit Paradis* and *Patrick O'Hara Creative Portrait*.

Radio includes Company 3 for Bristol Old Vic Archive.

### **Nadine Rennie CDG** | Casting Director

Nadine is Co-Chair of the Casting Directors Guild and Creative Associate at Synergy Theatre Project. Previously Nadine was Casting Director at Soho Theatre for over fifteen years.

Current projects include *The Pitchfork Disney* (King's Head Theatre); *Elmet* (Javaad Alipoor Company/Bradford 2025); *Lifers* (Southwark Playhouse); *Scenes From The Climate Era* (Gate Theatre) and *Dracapella* (Park Theatre).

Previous theatre includes *Providers* (Brixton House); *Expendable* (Royal Court Theatre); *Miracle on 34$^{th}$ Street* (HOME Manchester); *Pig Heart Boy* (Unicorn Theatre/UK tour); *Wish You Were Here* (Gate Theatre); *The Flea* (Yard Theatre); *My Mother's Funeral: The Show* and *Run Sister Run* (Paines Plough); *Leaves of Glass* and *Miss Julie* (Park Theatre); *Dead Girls Rising* (Silent Uproar); *We Could All Be Perfect*, *Typical Girls* and *The Last King of Scotland* (Sheffield Theatres); *He Said She Said* (Kiln Theatre); *Wreckage* and *Breeding* (King's Head Theatre); *Further Than The Furthest Thing* (Minack Theatre); *SHED: Exploded View* (Royal Exchange Theatre); *Bacon* (Finborough Theatre); *Es & Flo* (WMC/Kiln Theatre); *The Ministry of Lesbian Affairs* and *Super High Resolution* (Soho Theatre); *Britannicus* (Lyric Hammersmith); *The Breach* (Hampstead Theatre); *Little Baby Jesus* (Orange Tree Theatre) and *There Are No Beginnings* (Leeds Playhouse).

### **Chris Foxon** | Producer

Chris is Executive Director of Papatango and was named in *The Stage* 25.

Papatango productions include *The Watch House* (UK tour); *Some Demon* (Arcola Theatre/Bristol Old Vic); *Old Bridge* (winner of the Olivier Award for Outstanding Achievement in Affiliate Theatre, Bush Theatre); *Some of Us Exist in the Future, The Silence and the Noise* and *Ghost Stories from an Old Country* (UK tour); *Shook* (Southwark Playhouse/ UK tour; also broadcast on Sky Arts); *The Funeral Director* (Southwark Playhouse/UK tour); *Hanna* (Arcola Theatre/ UK tour); *Here, Trestle, Orca* and *Tomcat* (Southwark Playhouse); *After Independence* (winner of the Alfred Fagon Audience Award, Arcola Theatre/BBC Radio 4) and *Coolatully, Unscorched, Pack* and *Everyday Maps for Everyday Use* (Finborough Theatre).

Chris's other productions include *The Transatlantic Commissions* (Old Vic); *Donkey Heart* (Old Red Lion Theatre/West End); *The Fear of Breathing* (Finborough Theatre/Akasaka Red Theatre, Tokyo); *The Keepers of Infinite Space* (Park Theatre) and *Happy New* (West End).

He wrote *The Watch House* (UK tour; published by Bloomsbury) and is co-author of *Being A Playwright: A Career Guide For Writers*.

Chris is a trustee of Novo Theatre in his native Northumberland. A graduate of both Oxford University and the Royal Central School of Speech and Drama, he has lectured at these institutions and many others.

### Joshua Goodman | Producer

Joshua is Producer and Programmer at Park Theatre. A multidisciplinary theatre-maker, writer, composer and creative producer, his work has been described as 'genuinely euphoric' (*The Guardian*) and 'charmingly perfect' (*KulturFreak*).

Recent theatre includes *Perfect Show For Rachel* (Barbican Centre/Brighton Festival/ILT Festival; OffWestEnd Award Winner); *My Life As a Cowboy* (Omnibus Theatre); *Night Shift* (Zoo Co); *Twelfth Night, The Tempest* and *Live Bolero* (Nottingham Playhouse); *She Loves Me* (Sheffield Theatres); *Something Special* (Birmingham Rep); *The Jungle Book* and *Lysistrata* (Lakeside Arts); *Pygmalion* (English Theatre Frankfurt); *Operation Hummingbird, The Firework Maker's Daughter* and *The Beggars of York* (York Theatre Royal); *Valuable* (Mind The Gap); *She Was Walking Home, Colder Than Here* and *Any Mother Would* (Next Door

But One); *Cinderella* (Queen's Theatre, Hornchurch); *Moby Dick* (UK tour) and *Home Sweet Home* (Freedom Studios/ UK tour).

Film includes *See You Next Saturday* and *Heat*.

Josh is also a dramaturg and theatre historian, earning a PhD on the relationship between Broadway, Hollywood and the London stage. He has lectured at NYU, University of Southern California, Great American Songbook Foundation, Academy of Motion Picture Arts and Sciences, BFI and King's College London. He is an Advanced Member of *Book, Music and Lyrics*, London's only professional musical theatre writing workshop.

**Matthew Carnazza** | Lighting Programmer & Production Electrician

Matt trained at Rose Bruford College.

Theatre as lighting designer includes *Restless Natives* (Leith Theatre); *Shock Horror* (UK tour); *The Light House* (Leeds Playhouse/UK tour); *Tomorrow Is Already Dead* (Soho Theatre/Hackney Showrooms); *Force of Nature* (international tour) and *122 Love Stories* (Harrogate Theatre).

Theatre as associate/programmer includes *A Thousand Splendid Suns* (Birmingham Rep/UK tour); *National Youth Dance Company* (Sadler's Wells/UK tour); *Nutcracker* (Southbank Centre); *The Clothes They Stood Up In* (Nottingham Playhouse); *All Blood Runs Red*, *Now*, *ALiCE* and *Here & Now* (UK tours); *Here* (Southwark Playhouse); *Old Bridge* (Bush Theatre) and *Some Demon* (Arcola Theatre/Bristol Old Vic).

Matt has also been Technical Manager for Jasmin Vardimon Company, Sadler's Wells, Imitating the Dog and DanceCity.

**2024 Papatango New Writing Prize Reading Team** |
Olu Alakija, Lucy Allan, Folabomi Amuludun, Ayad Andrews, Robert Awosusi, Robyn Bennett, Joanna Bowman, Alice Chambers, Laura Clifford, Lou Corben, Bridie Donaghy, Sofia Gallucci-Giles, Sarah Garrett, Antonia Georgieva, Harry Gould, Karis Kelly, Shabnom Khanom, Julia Levai, Gemma Murray, Louis Shankar, William Byam Shaw, Luna Mia Sigle, Sarah Stacey, Blythe Stewart, Krystal Sweedman, Adam Tutt, Katie Weatherill, Emma Wilkinson, Beth Wilson, Matt Woodhead and Rosie Wyatt

**Graphic Design** | William Andrews for Team Wonderful & Doug Kerr for Studio Doug

**Press Representation** | Kate Morley PR

**R&D Cast** | Joana Borja, Marcello Cruz, Stuart McQuarrie, Pooky Quesnel and Jamael Westman

Many thanks to the 2024 Papatango New Writing Prize's generous supporters: Amazon Literary Partnership; Backstage Trust; Boris Karloff Charitable Foundation; Fenton Arts Trust; Foyle Foundation; Garfield Weston Foundation; Golsoncott Foundation; Harold Hyam Wingate Foundation; Katie Bradford Arts Trust; Maria Bjornson Memorial Fund.

Finally, the producers express their profound gratitude to New York's **Immigrant Defense Project** for their advice and for the work they do to protect vulnerable communities.

The Immigrant Defense Project was founded in New York following harsh 1996 laws that vastly expanded the government's power to arrest and deport our neighbours who are not citizens, in particular by using deeply unjust systems of policing and incarceration. Ever since, the IDP has been fighting for immigrants using a multipronged strategy which includes advocacy and shaping policy, direct legal assistance and support, training and education, challenges to unfair laws through impact litigation, and changing hearts and minds through narrative change. They are committed to a basic principle: all human beings deserve dignity – and nobody is disposable.

**'Remarkable unearthers of new talent.'** *Evening Standard*

Papatango is an Olivier Award-winning theatre company whose leadership team was named in *The Stage* 25 list of theatre-makers shaping the industry. We provide pathways for artists and audiences otherwise without access to professional theatre. Our opportunities are free and open to everyone.

The Papatango New Writing Prize was the UK's first award to guarantee a debut playwright a full production, publication, royalties and commission. All other entrants receive feedback on their scripts. 1,589 entries were received in 2024, meaning the Prize continues to average more annual submissions than any other UK playwriting scheme – and yet uniquely gives support to all.

Other opportunities include touring productions with community partnerships; bespoke digital platforms offering training, funding and industry representation; and GoWrite, a creative writing programme transforming vulnerable young people in state schools, pupil referral units, SEN centres and refugee, mental health or care settings into produced and published playwrights. We support over 6,000 people each year.

Writers launched by Papatango have won BAFTA, Olivier, Critics' Circle, *The Times* Breakthrough, OffWestEnd, RNT Foundation Playwright and Alfred Fagon Awards, premiering in 33 countries.

Our motto is simple: all you need is a story.

**Artistic Director** George Turvey
**Executive Director** Chris Foxon
**Creative Learning & Engagement Producer** Kate Ereira

**Board**
Stephanie Bain (Chair)
Fezzan Ahmed
Serena Basra
Sally Cookson
Sam Donovan
Davina Moss
Nicholas Rogers
Tom Wright

# PARK THEATRE

★★★★★ "A five-star neighbourhood theatre"
*Independent*

Park Theatre was founded by Artistic Director, Jez Bond and Creative Director Emeritus, Melli Marie. The building opened in May 2013 and, with 10 West End transfers (including *Rose* starring Maureen Lipman, *The Boys in the Band* starring Mark Gatiss and *Pressure* starring David Haig), two National Theatre transfers, an RSC transfer and 14 national tours in its first 12 years, has garnered a reputation as a key player in the London theatre scene. Park Theatre has been awarded numerous Offie Awards, West End Wilma's Accessible Theatre Award, The Stage's Fringe Theatre of the Year and Campaign of the Year Awards, as well as receiving seven Olivier Award nominations.

We are a welcoming and accessible venue, delivering work of exceptional calibre in the heart of Finsbury Park. We work with brilliant writers, directors and artists to present compelling, exciting and beautifully told stories in our two intimate spaces. Our programme focuses on new writing and revivals of modern classics, alongside a commitment to presenting joyful, entertaining shows for audiences from all walks of life. We produce our own shows, as well as working in partnership with emerging and established theatre producers. We contribute to the broader theatre industry by offering mentoring, support and opportunities to artists.

Our Creative Engagement programmes seek to widen the number and range of people who participate in creative activities, and provide opportunities for those with little or no prior contact with the arts. In everything we do we aim to be warm and inclusive; a safe, welcoming and wonderful space to work, create and visit. Park Theatre has been accredited by the Mayor of London as a Dementia Friendly building.

As a registered charity with no regular public subsidy, we rely on the kind support of our donors and volunteers. To find out how you can get involved visit parktheatre.co.uk, or scan this QR code

**Park Theatre**

Artistic Director
Jez Bond

Executive Director
Catherine McKinney

**Artistic**
Producer and Programmer
Joshua Goodman

Producing and Programme Coordinator
Ellen Harris

**Creative Engagement**
Creative Engagement Manager
Carys Rose Thomas

**Development**
Development Manager (Individuals)
Alannah Lewis

**Finance**
Finance Director
Elaine Lavelle

Finance Officer
Nicola Brown

Finance Assistant
Pinar Kurdik

**General Management**
General Manager
Tom Bailey

Deputy General Manager
David Hunter

Administrator
Mariah Sayer

Duty Venue Managers
Amber De Ruyt, Leiran Gibson, Zara Naeem, Laura Riseborough, David Hunter, Shaun Joynson & Wayne Morris

**Park Pizza**
Supervisors
Toby Schuster & Alistair Bourne

Team Members
George Gehm, Bradly Doko, Jordon Goodlitt, Maddie Stoneman, Ruairi McGonagle, Saron Tariku, Harry Taylor, Benjamin McCann, Owen McCabe, Tessa Doubleday, Anika McIntosh & Ewan Brand

**Sales & Marketing**
Sales & Marketing Director
Dawn James

Sales & Marketing Director (Maternity Cover)
Nicci Allt

Head of Ticketing
Matthew Barker

Sales & Ticketing Manager
Lou Egan

Marketing Manager
Monique Walker

Marketing Officer
Eliza Jones

Box Office Supervisors
Jacquie Cassidy, Belinda Clark, Natasha Green, Gareth Hackney & Maddie Stoneman

Public Relations
Mobius Industries

**Technical & Building**
Technical & Building Manager
Gianluca Zona

Deputy Technical & Building Manager
Teddy Nash

Venue Technician
Michael Bird

**Trustees**
Anthony Clare (Chair)
Jonathan Edwards (Vice Chair)
Ibukun Alamutu
Professor Kurt Barling
Hedda Beeby
Kathleen Heycock
Jacqueline Hurt
Joe Smith
Julia Tyrrell
Pia Richards-Glöckner

Founding President | Jeremy Bond † (1939–2020)

With thanks to all our supporters, donors and volunteers.

# THE MEAT KINGS! (INC.) OF BROOKLYN HEIGHTS

Hannah Doran

## Acknowledgements

Thank you to Papatango Theatre Company (George Turvey, Chris Foxon, Kate Ereira) for supporting emerging playwrights and taking big risks on new writing – I couldn't have asked for better people to guide my debut play into production. Thanks also to all the readers of the 2024 Papatango Prize.

Thank you to Jez Bond, Catherine McKinney, Joshua Goodman, and everyone at Park Theatre for your willingness – and more so, your eagerness – to engage with debut plays and playwrights, and for championing this play.

Thank you to the creatives and crew who brought this butchers to life. What an incredible team. George in particular was an extraordinary dramaturg, director, and collaborator.

Thank you to Kate Morley, Cameron Currie and James Butterworth for your marvellous PR.

I began writing *The Meat Kings!* during the 2020 lockdown, as part of an online writers' group run by The Shelter theatre company in New York. I am grateful to all those writers for showing up despite everything going on in the world, and in particular to Ryan and Rochelle, who read my pages long after the group had ended.

Thank you to Jacob Marx Rice, for your insatiable excitement about the bare bones of this story, and for your shrewd notes. Thank you to Charles Gershman, who championed this play from afar and generously produced a reading via Zoom so that I could hear it aloud for the very first time.

Thank you to the many actors whose readings and perspectives formed essential parts of the play's development: Judy del Giudice (my mentor and friend), Rolls Andre, Chad Anthony Miller, Ricardo Lopez Montilla, Jeremy Suarez, Danny Tejera, Emily Verla, Joana Borja, Stuart McQuarrie, Pooky Quesnel, and Jamael Westman; and thank you to our unreal world premiere company: Jackie Clune, Marcello Cruz, Ash Hunter, Mithra Malek, and Eugene McCoy.

This play would not exist without the meat-cutting team I was fortunate to be a part of in Brooklyn. Thank you to the leaders and friends who made it joyful – Emily, Massimo, Dustin, Eddie, Tristan, Rachel – and all the rest. I wouldn't have wanted to be elbow deep in chicken at five a.m. with anyone else.

Thank you to Laura Waldren, Stewart Pringle, Samuel Bailey, and Simon Stephens for your thoughtful guidance.

Thank you to Jessy Roberts and the reading panel at the National Theatre Studio – the ultimate hype team.

Thank you to Lynne Davis.

Thank you to all my wonderful bookselling family.

Thank you to Philippa and Michael; Adam, Corey, Ellen, Fern, Gilles, Karishma, Kerry, Laura, Logan, Nicola, Sally Cade, Sam, Sophia.

Thank you to Alden Sargent for your story-brain, most brilliant notes, and top-tier bromance.

Thank you, Kate, for believing in me, in success and in failure.

And for your faith no matter what, for your sacrifices and unconditional love, thank you to my family. Mum, Dad and Alex. And Tara and Cassie.

*H.D.*

## Characters

T, *early twenties. Female. Any ethnicity. Quiet, guarded, diligent. Newly on the straight and narrow. Billy's cousin.*

BILLY, *thirties. Apprentice Butcher. Mixed race (written here as half Irish American and half Dominican, but this can be changed according to casting needs and/or storytelling preference). Tattooed. A pussycat usually, but did two years for assault; he's pretty chill, but boy, you would not fuck with him. T's cousin.*

JUAN DIEGO, *or* JD, *nineteen/twenty. Apprentice Butcher. Mexican, Brooklyn-raised. Just trying to get along in life. Fits in wherever he goes.*

PAULA, *forties – sixties. Italian American. Store owner. Butch dyke, major swag. Always jovial but undeniably The Boss. She gets it done; no time for these boys and their bullshit.*

DAVID, *forties – fifties. Caucasian. Head Butcher. Ex-Wall Street guy. Used to take care of himself but has let that go a little.*

## Notes

Where the end of a line has no punctuation, this is meant to capture the nature of real speech and conversation, of thoughts that aren't necessarily complete or final.

An ellipsis (…) indicates a longer pause.

A forward slash ( / ) indicates an active interruption or crossing over of speech.

*This text went to press before the end of rehearsals and so may differ slightly from the play as performed.*

## Pre-Set

*The storefront of a butchers in Williamsburg, Brooklyn, New York.*

*Large bay windows, one side displaying dry-aged meats, the other, cured meats and salamis hanging on racks.*

*The door, with a long window, is slightly ajar.*

*Above, a sign reading:*

*'Cafarelli & Sons. Meat Market. Est. 1925.'*

*Peeling dark green paint. A faded awning folded away.*

*Red, white and blue fourth of July decorations – bunting, streamers or wreaths – hang from the awning, and a large banner or poster reading:*

*'Happy 4th! Celebrating 100 years of Cafarelli's. Great deals inside for the holiday weekend.'*

*The door swings gently in the breeze. The bell jingles.*

## ACT ONE

### Scene One

*Lights up. The storefront rises and reveals:*

*The windowless back cut room of the butchers.*

*White subway tile goes halfway up the walls, some with small blood splatters.*

*Steel workstations line the walls, with another centre like an island. Large white cut-boards on top and cupboards or open storage underneath.*

*Back wall: carts and tray racks, and a large steel sink.*

*Upstage: metal meat hooks hang from a ceiling rail, half a pig carcass slung up on one.*

*Stage right: a coat rack and bag storage, whites and aprons rack, and swing doors leading to the store and the office offstage right.*

*Stage left: more cupboard and worktop space, and swing doors which lead to:*

*Offstage left, unseen, a grinder, a bandsaw, and other equipment, and the walk-in chiller.*

*8 a.m., 4th July.*

*Loud music.*

BILLY, DAVID, *and* JUAN DIEGO *prepare meat.* DAVID *and* JD *cut different steaks,* BILLY *twists sausages. They all wear white jackets and red aprons, and store-branded caps or beanies.*

*– Always, during the dialogue, they're cutting, or preparing something. If they stop, it's for a reason. Anytime anyone turns, there's probably a knife in their hand.*

*They are focused and fast, but they also sing along.* BILLY *hits skip and the song changes to Latin pop.* JUAN DIEGO *shuffles his feet. Then his butt. Then he dances properly, salsa-ing with an invisible woman. He's a good dancer.*

DAVID. What's her name, JD?

BILLY. *His* name, more like it, what's *his* name

> JD, *unfazed, shimmies his ass up towards* BILLY.

Get outta here!

> BILLY *pushes* JD *away and turns the music down.*

JD. Aw, you don't wanna dance?

BILLY. Here, I'll give you something to dance with

*He slides the half-pig carcass down the rail towards* JD, *who catches it.*

JD. Oh hey baby, *mi amor,* you smell so good

DAVID. Bill, you gave him your girl! That's so nice of you, what a nice gift

*JD slides the carcass back towards* BILLY.

*The sound of the bell as the shop door opens.* PAULA *enters, sunglasses on at first. She has cups of coffee, which the guys take, and a bag of pastries.*

PAULA. Morning, fuckers. Happy Fourth. Alright. Milk one sugar. Milk two sugars. Cream four sugars. And one for me.

DAVID. Extra black, extra no sugar?

JD. Oof, bitterrrrrrr

PAULA. I'm a very bitter woman, JD. And I brought you some holiday breakfast out of the goodness of my cold bitter heart.

*On a clean counter, she rips open the pastry bag.* JD *goes and peers into the bag.*

JD. Ohhh, what do we got – here Bill

ACT ONE, SCENE ONE 9

JD *tosses a small pastry which* BILLY *catches in his mouth.* PAULA *passes a pastry to* DAVID. DAVID *wipes his bloody knife on his apron and holds it out for* PAULA *to slide the pastry on it.*

PAULA. Absolutely not.

DAVID *laughs, removes his glove and goes over to take the pastry.*

JD. No almond croissant? For real?

PAULA. Hey, take what you get. Alright guys, I really appreciate you being here today. We're gonna be rammed, so stack it high. And I want meat on sticks. If it can go on a stick, put it on a stick. Chicken, lamb, steaks. Kabob it up. People love that shit. Alright?

DAVID. Yep

BILLY. You got it

PAULA. Good. Our new summer temp starts today, I want you setting a good example so clean your benches please. Bill, can you prep the grinder ready for open?

BILLY. I already did that, boss

PAULA. Oh yeah?

DAVID *nods, confirming.*

Nice. I like this new side of you, Bill. Alright, could you sweep the floor please?

BILLY. Oh sure thing, boss

PAULA *tosses him a broom and exits.*

Motherf–

JD. What?

BILLY. She always pickin' on me

DAVID. Aw you don't wanna sweep?

BILLY. I don't want her up my ass in front of T

JD. Who's T?

DAVID. That's right, you know the new guy

JD. Oh yeah, Paula said it's your friend. Damn bro these nemo babies

DAVID. Ne*po*

BILLY. It's not my *kid* –

JD. Imagine

DAVID. Bill Junior

BILLY. – And it's not a new guy, it's a new *girl*

JD. It's a what

DAVID. Oh you're bringing girls in here now?

JD. No he's *not*

   *Beat.*

   …Bill don't know no girls

   BILLY *gives him a shove, they tussle briefly.*

BILLY. Oh yeah? You got a lot of girls, huh? You gettin' some huh? Nah bro she's my *cousin*

DAVID. Oh, okay, that's nice, family connection

JD. Is she like your cousin though or like, your cousin

BILLY. She's my cousin, bro, and she lives with me, so you don't even think about it, how's that

JD. Aright I'm not thinkin' nothin'

DAVID. Get sweeping, Bill. I told you, you want that JC, you gotta do the dirty work.

BILLY. Dirty work's all I'm doin'!

JD. Sweep bitch

   BILLY *shoves him again, then half-heartedly sweeps.*
   DAVID, *observing* JD *cutting:*

DAVID. Here. Try this one.

*He hands him a different knife.*

They're just a little uneven. See? You wanna keep it… like this. The knife up, like that.

BILLY. He getting special treatment?

DAVID. I'm training both of you remember

BILLY. You don't teach me shit

*This isn't true, and* DAVID *is affronted.*

DAVID. Alright. Do the other half of that rib for me.

*He holds out the knife.* BILLY *pauses.*

BILLY. I don't… I didn't finish sweeping yet. JD you wanna swap?

JD. I'm good bro

DAVID. Later, when it's quiet. We'll work on something. Okay?

BILLY *drags the broom offstage left.*

(*To* JD.) Yeah, nice. So then when you come to the bone it's nice and clean and you can saw right through. Yeah. Perfect. See? What am I?

JD. Good at what you / do.

DAVID. / Good at what I do. Damn right.

JD. Was that your catchphrase on Wall Street too, Bernie?

DAVID. No, FUCK YOU. That was my catchphrase.

*The sound of the bell, and* PAULA*'s voice, 'Hi! Welcome!' They stop cutting, try to listen.*

She's getting the grilling.

JD. It's not a girl, man

DAVID. He said it's a girl

JD. He's fuckin with us, it's not a girl

DAVID. It might be a girl

JD. It's not a girl! Like Bill just knows a girl cutter?

DAVID. He said it's his cousin

JD. How many woman butchers you seen in your life?

DAVID. Some…

JD. It would be nice if it was. I mean – just like, nice, you know, different

DAVID. Ehhh…

> DAVID*'s not enamoured with the idea.* BILLY *re-enters without the broom.*

Anyway girls are scared of Paula

JD. *I'm* scared of Paula

BILLY. Come on

JD. I'm scared of Paula like, like I was scared of my mom

DAVID. You're *still* scared of your mom

BILLY. He's scared of all girls

JD. Yo shut up

BILLY. You are, I seen you, I seen you

> *They tussle,* BILLY *teasing him.* PAULA *enters with* T *and they get back to work.*

PAULA. Maybe you can help me keep these guys in check. As you can see they sometimes get a little carried away. What did I just say? Come on. Hands move faster than mouths. Alright guys. This is T. She's gonna be working with us.

*Beat.*

> BILLY *and* T *share a nod or smile.* JD *turns to* DAVID *and* BILLY.

JD. It *is a girl*

ACT ONE, SCENE ONE 13

PAULA. Thank you JD for your astute observations. T will be here full-time till Labor Day. I know I don't have to tell you to be nice to her. T, I'm gonna pair you up with Juan Diego. I want you guys making patties. Okay?

BILLY. I actually made like a hundred patties already, boss

PAULA. Great, you want a medal? It's the biggest grilling day of the year. You can marinade some chicken for kabobs.

BILLY. But I –

PAULA. There's two vats of thighs in the cooler. Barbecue dry rub and do some lemon pepper as well. Opening soon guys, get your shit ready.

PAULA *exits. A moment of silence. Then* JD *waves awkwardly at* T *before ripping off his glove and shaking her hand.*

JD. Hi. I'm – hello – Juan Di – JD. Good to meet you.

T. T.

JD. JD.

T. Yeah you said.

BILLY. Jesus bro, cool off. Yowassup my sis

T. Hey J – I mean –

JD. J?

BILLY. I told you, nobody calls me that here

T. Sorry. Billy.

DAVID. Bill's not your name?

BILLY. It's my middle name, after my dad.

JD. What's your real name

T. Jésus

DAVID. The fuck

JD. *Jésus?? No manches* [No way]

BILLY. Come on do I really look like a Billy to you? Yeah someone started using it while I was inside. He said to me I can't be named after Jesus after what I did, it was too ironical or whatever so I got Billy'd and it stuck

JD. *Güey* [Bro], that's wild.

BILLY. Anyway that's Dave, he's Head Chop

DAVID. Hello

T. Hey

BILLY. Also known as Bernie

DAVID. Nope

BILLY. And I guess you guys are making patties

JD. Yeah, let's get you a jacket.

*He takes her to the whites/apron rack and rifles through.*

You're definitely gonna be a small. Maybe extra small but I don't think we have those. How much do you weigh, if you don't mind me asking?

DAVID. JD

JD. What?

DAVID. You can't ask a girl that

JD. Oh I'm sorry… uh. You handled meat before?

T. A little

BILLY. She definitely has

DAVID *and* JD *snigger.*

T. Hey shut it

JD. Oh I – sorry –

T. Not you

BILLY. Alright my bad

JD. Anyway. Uh. Everyone has their own knife set. You can share mine today. And you'll need a cut glove. Lemme have a look. Probably a small too…

JD *looks in a box of gloves for a small.*

DAVID. Ten bucks Paula does her history speech before we open

JD. Here we go!

*He hands her a glove.*

BILLY (*to* DAVID). Nah man not today, it's too busy

JD. Okay. Let's – we're gonna make some patties – and show you how we do things here. So you – you *have* worked with meat before

T. Yeah

JD *fetches some ingredients.*

BILLY. Dreamer boy here's also an Apprentice, T, same as me

JD. Yeah. We got our cut tests coming up in a couple weeks. Then we'll be Junior Cutters.

(*He glances at* BILLY.) If we pass.

DAVID. You'll pass.

BILLY. Oh, thanks

DAVID. You'll pass too. Third time's the charm.

T. Junior Cutter. That's cool.

JD. Yeah. Anyway – here

*He lifts a very heavy vat of ground beef, and struggles.*

T. Oh – let me help

JD. It's cool it's – not heavy at all – I got it

*He sets it down.*

So this is easy. You just use the patty moulds, mix whatever you want into the grinds and that's it. Maybe start with cheese and bacon bits. Then you can eat the cheese and bacon bits.

*He does so. But she dives right in and gets to work, mixing in the seasonings and making patties, churning them out at alarming speed into a stack, smoothly tearing parchment paper for between each layer.* JD *watches and looks at* BILLY.

PAULA *enters.*

PAULA. Some sliders would be great too, JD – come on guys I got a half empty display case out there. This is a big day for us, I'm not trying to lose all my business to Whole Foods here, alright?

BILLY. Yes boss

*They get going.* PAULA *goes to the pork bench and starts preparing ribs.*

JD. Hey not bad, Paula!

PAULA. What's that?

JD. She's alright.

PAULA. Yeah, did you think I was gonna bring a first-timer in on the fourth of July?

JD. ...No.

PAULA. So T while we're here, why don't I fill you in on the history of our store?

DAVID. Called it

JD. Nailed it

BILLY. Goddamnit Dave

*He passes* DAVID *ten bucks.*

PAULA. It's important to understand what you're working for, no? You've come in on our centenary. Cafarelli and Sons has been open for a hundred years this year, it's a big milestone for us. My great-great-grandfather came to New York from Sicily in –

DAVID / JD. 1913.

PAULA. – 1913, thank you boys. You know the Meatpacking District? Pretty fancy these days but back then it was like slaughterhouse central.

JD. And she always thinks the clue's in the name – Meatpacking

DAVID. – but people are often surprised to hear that!

PAULA. ... I always think the clue's in the name but people are often surprised by that. And he – Sal Cafarelli – worked there, firstly slaughtering, cutting meat, then packing meat, all kinds of things – till he could afford to open his own butchers – tiny store a few blocks down, near Lorimer. It used to be a laundromat, now it's condos. Then he bought this place in...?

*This time she gives them a chance to chip in.*

DAVID / JD. May 1925.

PAULA. May 1925, exactly. He opened in July that year. And it was very successful. Eventually he passed the business down to his son –

DAVID / JD. – Sal –

PAULA. – who passed it to his son

DAVID / JD. – Sal –

PAULA. – thank you, yes – who passed it to my dad –

DAVID / JD. – Sal –

PAULA. – who passed it to me.

DAVID / JD. – Paula!

PAULA. And here we are a hundred years later, still thriving, still selling the finest meats to our local community. We've always said it, we are the living embodiment of the American Dream.

DAVID. Hell yeah!

PAULA. And we're ve–

JD. – thrilled to have you join us.

DAVID. Overjoyed.

PAULA. I wouldn't have said 'thrilled' or 'overjoyed' but the sentiment's the same. Glad to have you. I expect a good attitude, I expect you to show up on time, I expect the same hard work my own ancestors put in.

T. Yes ma'am.

PAULA. And you picked a helluva day to start. KABOBS, guys. Move it!

*PAULA exits with her tray of ribs.*

JD. So there ya go

T. Wow

*BILLY sighs.*

BILLY. Fuckin chicken, man

DAVID. What'd I tell ya? Pollo asado, amigo. – It's mostly bullshit, by the way.

*BILLY exits.*

JD. What is

DAVID. Paula's dad was on his deathbed when he finally signed the business over to her. She only got it because her brothers didn't want it.

JD. Don't be a dick, Bernie

DAVID. What, it's true

T. So how many of these, exactly

JD. Oh. Infinite.

*She raises her eyebrows.*

Just like – infinite. Just keep going.

T. Really?

JD. She wasn't joking. By this afternoon they'll all be gone. Though if there's any left she'll probably let us take them

ACT ONE, SCENE ONE   19

home for free, so yeah. Make a ton and you'll have burgers till Thanksgiving!

(*Awkwardly, as she doesn't reply.*) You… you like burgers?

T. Sure.

JD. I mean yeah, of course you do. Is there anything you haven't cut before?

T. Yeah. Some of those cuts out there – I haven't even heard of them.

JD. Oh no worries, we'll teach you everything. Do you like cooking? Paula likes it, when you learn to cut something new, if you try cooking it, or at least taste it.

T. Oh. Uh.

JD. I mean it's not like, required, like homework, or anything.

DAVID (*teasing* JD). But I bet if you ask JD nicely he might cook you up a little something. Maybe do a dance for you while you wait

JD *glares at him.* DAVID *loads up trays and carries them off.*

T. A dance?

JD. I dance a little, yeah. I'll teach you that too.

T. Oh, I –

JD. But yeah I love cooking. And eating. I'm gonna go to the grills in the park after work, with some friends – we're gonna cook up some ribs, go to the batting cages, throw a ball around, you know – you can totally come if you want, we can get a little extra for you

T. I can't. But thanks.

JD. Yeah, you probably have plans, it was stupid

T. No! It wasn't. I love baseball

JD. You do??

DAVID *enters, holds the door open.*

DAVID. T – Paula needs you for a sec

> T *heads for the door.*

JD. Wait – the most important question of all. Yankees?

T. Mets.

JD. WHAT.

DAVID. *Nice*

> DAVID *high fives* T *as she exits.* DAVID *lets the door swing shut and pointedly stares at* JD.

JD. What? What?? She seems cool

DAVID. Oh yeah? *Cool* huh?

> BILLY *enters with a huge vat of chicken, and sets it down on the island.*

BILLY. Aright, your boy marinaded

JD. Shut up! I'm not even tryna

DAVID (*in a goofy, mocking voice*). Hi there hello I'm JD it's good to / meet you

BILLY (*not missing a beat, in the same voice, shaking* DAVID's *hand*). So great it's the best day of my life I'm almost the Junior Cutter / and a huge kiss-ass

DAVID. / please um tell me what's your exact height / and weight please

JD. / Are you done? Are you finished?

> BILLY *and* DAVID *laugh. Maybe* BILLY *comes close to* JD. *There's a brief hint of danger.*

BILLY. Aright, aright. But I'm just sayin', dreamer. You better not.

JD. It's all good, bro, chill. Damn.

> JD *exits.*

DAVID. Alright get that chicken on sticks and in some trays. I'm gonna get the beef set out.

BILLY. Uh huh

DAVID. What you doing tonight?

BILLY. Not much. Chillin. Fourth tastes different when you been inside, you know?

DAVID. Uh huh. Feels good, doesn't it

BILLY. Got some beers in the cooler. Gonna smoke a little L. Cook something for my mom.

DAVID. Oh yeah how's she

BILLY. I tell you it's spread? It's in her lungs now too.

DAVID. Shit. I'm sorry

BILLY. They're trying her on a new medication – a trial. It gives her night terrors. She's moaning and sweating all night. And I went in there, lifted her head to put a washcloth on her neck, her hair's coming out in my hands.

DAVID. Fuck.

BILLY. I gotta pass this test, man, I need that raise.

DAVID. Well you gotta keep showing her you want it. Pull your finger out, man

BILLY. I know, I know. What you doing later?

DAVID. Oh you know. Not blowing coke. Not talking to my kids. Not jumping off the Brooklyn Bridge.

BILLY. Nice.

DAVID. Yup.

BILLY. ...You wanna come by? I got a bottle of tequila needs drinking

DAVID. Oh, nah – I... I mean. Sure, man, if you –

BILLY. Yeah bro, no problem. Is America's birthday we gotta get the guys together right, have some Buds for your guy Ralph

DAVID. Hey thanks man, that's really nice.

BILLY. I gotchu

*They fist bump.* DAVID *exits with trays.*

*Beat.* BILLY *looks about. He takes off his gloves. He exits and then re-enters with several packs of meat. He goes to his bag in the corner and puts the packs in the bag.*

DAVID *re-enters and goes to his bench, followed by* JD *who removes his apron and jacket.* BILLY *straightens up quickly and steps awkwardly away from the bag.*

DAVID. Gimme a hand with this would you?

JD. Nah man I'm takin my break before it gets too busy

DAVID *(to* BILLY*)*. …What you doing?

BILLY. Nothin' – lemme help

BILLY *goes to help* DAVID *lift a heavy vat, but instead takes the whole thing himself.* JD *exits with a:*

JD. Alright, later

DAVID. Bring me back an almond croissant

BILLY. Yeah bring us a croissant, kiss-ass

JD. No problem, Jésus

BILLY. Ey shut the hell up – get the door, Bernie

DAVID. What did we say about that

DAVID *holds the door for* BILLY *and both exit.*

*Blackout.*


### Scene Two

*Later.*

*The shop is about to close. It's slower, chill.* T *sharpens knives and puts them away.* BILLY *cleans surfaces and chats to* DAVID*, who ties a pork shoulder.* T *watches* DAVID *out of the corner of her eye.*

BILLY. You're a disloyal motherfucker

DAVID. What can I say, the Knicks sucked when I jumped ship, now they're back on form

BILLY. You just wanna back whoever's winning

DAVID. Well losing's no fun. By law you should be a Nets fan anyway, that's your birthright. You're not a Manhattan boy

BILLY. My girlfriend lived in Murray Hill

DAVID. You don't have a girlfriend

BILLY. My *ex*-girlfriend

JD *enters with trays of steaks.*

DAVID. Just because the nineteen-year-old you were boning lived in Murray Hill doesn't make *you* a Manhattanite

BILLY. So maybe I *identify* as a Manhattanite

JD. For a lot of reasons I think that's the worst thing you've ever said

T *laughs;* JD *is delighted.*

DAVID. You're not a Manhattanite. In your dreams.

BILLY. Nah Bernie, in yours. – That's a lot of steaks, bro

JD. Yeah she's not happy. And these are turning. Gonna have to grind 'em in the morning. I was right though T – patties till Thanksgiving

*He holds up a tray of patties that haven't sold.*

BILLY. I told her, I told her it was too many

T. Hey what is that? Pork butt?

DAVID. Pork *shoulder*.

T. Oh. What are you doing with it?

DAVID. It's called BRT. You know what that is?

BILLY *snorts.*

BILLY. Hell yeah, tied rolled n boned baby, just how I like her

JD *and* BILLY *share a snicker.*

DAVID. BRT. Boned, rolled, and tied. You de-bone the shoulder, roll it nice and tight, and tie it, that's all.

T. And you're using different knives?

DAVID. Well they're all for different things, so…

*PAULA sticks her head in.*

PAULA. Dave can you do me some flat iron?

DAVID. Uh I'm on pork right now

PAULA. Alright, I'll do it

*PAULA exits.*

T. What's the difference [in the knives]

DAVID. These are better for cutting around bone. This is JD's favourite –

*He holds up a knife. BILLY cracks up. JD knows where this is going.*

JD. – No it's not –

DAVID. – It's called a Six Inch Boner

*He and BILLY laugh.*

He likes to hold it

BILLY. It feels uh – aspirational

JD. Great. Great.

*They quieten as PAULA enters carrying some beef and lays it out on the central workstation. T ignores their banter.*

T. Can you show me?

DAVID. What's that? Oh. Uh. This is ready for a customer. Maybe another time.

BILLY. Man you spent too much time with kiss-ass dreamer today, T.

*T shrugs.*

ACT ONE, SCENE TWO 25

T. I just find it interesting

PAULA. You ever cut flat iron, T?

T. No

PAULA. Wanna try?

BILLY. Flat iron, that's some complex shit

PAULA. Just takes practice and confidence. In fact, all of you – come on.

BILLY. Paula it's four o'clock

PAULA. This'll be a fifty dollar sale. C'mon, I seem to remember flat irons tripped you up on your last cut test.

BILLY *begrudgingly gets his gloves on. JD joins.*

JD. I love doing these, it's so satisfying

*The three of them stand in a row and cut a steak each.* PAULA *guides them, mostly focusing on* T.

PAULA. Okay, so take your knife up top there, see that line of sinew, take your knife and just kind of peel it away – inside, that's it, JD… See that gristly stuff, now just keep doing that, all the way through, that's great, T, nice… Yep, follow the line – Bill keep it straight, gliding not hacking. Gliding not hacking. (*She momentarily puts her hands over* BILLY*'s.*) Make a – like an arc shape with the knife. Nice. That's it.

JD (*to* BILLY*, jokingly*). Cow's already dead, bro, what you trying to do to it

DAVID. Nice and gentle, Bill

PAULA. Be bold with the motion… Y'ever filleted a whole salmon? No? This is kinda like that, you don't wanna lose any good meat.

JD. *Only* Paula's out there buyin' whole ass salmons

PAULA. Keep going, slide through the end. Easy, Bill, alright. Then just take them apart. Yeah, not bad T.

JD (*hushed, awed, looking at T's work*). Shit. That's your first one?

PAULA. Then it's just the same thing for each piece, removing the sinew. But don't worry about that, I'll finish them up. Nice, JD. (*To* BILLY:) It won't cook evenly like that, we just wanna keep the knife nice and straight, alright? It's okay, don't worry about it

BILLY (*mumbling*). Fuck that stupid shit

> BILLY *throws his knife down, frustrated, and takes his jacket off. He's clearly pissed off.* PAULA *takes over the flat irons, tidying them up.* T *and* JD *also prepare to leave.*

JD. That was mad good, T – where'd you learn to cut like that?

BILLY. Prison.

JD. Oh. F'real?

T. Uh. Yeah.

JD. Oh, okay. Yo Paula she should get to take it home!

PAULA. Yeah… maybe you could settle for some unsold patties

JD. I'll buy it for her!

PAULA. Sure, it'll only cost you two hours' pay.

JD. Oh. Shit

T. That's ok, I don't want it

JD (*teasingly*). What, you don't like steak?

T. Not really

JD. What?! You prefer like, lamb or something?

T. No I – I just

BILLY. She doesn't eat meat.

JD. …Is that a joke?

> T *gives* BILLY *a look.*

T. No, it's not.

## ACT ONE, SCENE TWO 27

JD. Paula you hired a vegan butcher?

PAULA. That's a first

T. I'm not *vegan*

> PAULA *hands the wrapped steaks to* JD.

PAULA. Look I don't care if you don't eat it, as long as you can cut it. – He's waiting outside. Close the shutters for me, would ya?

JD. Yeah, no problem

PAULA. Thanks for today guys. I'll see ya.

> BILLY *exits, throwing the door open, putting a cigarette in his mouth as he goes.*

T. Thank you, it's been good.

PAULA. Thanks T. See you tomorrow.

JD (*to* T, *as they exit*). So what *do* you eat?

> DAVID *folds his arms and leans on the counter.* PAULA *cleans her board.*
>
> *A silence.*

DAVID. So. What'd we make?

PAULA. I don't know. I didn't check.

> *Not normal for* PAULA. DAVID *raises his eyebrows.*

DAVID. This morning was busy, at least.

PAULA. Busy. There used to be lines out the door on the fourth. I stopped by Jeff Bezos' Fine Meats on my lunch break, it was rammed.

DAVID. Whole Foods? Yeah they're selling frozen sausages, of course they're cheap… How bad is it?

> PAULA *waves him away.*

PAULA. It's fine. It's fine.

DAVID. Paula. I got eyes, I know it's bad. There's twenty pounds of patties that didn't sell. Two trays of sirloin. Four boxes of ribs... You've been here since 5 a.m. You're *here* sixty hours a week. You held off on hiring a new person till the actual fourth of July. Till we were basically desperate.

PAULA. I felt bad replacing Ralph

DAVID. Fuck Ralph. We needed someone. And then you hired *her* on a temp contract, not even permanent. And she's ...

PAULA *looks at him.*

She seems good, but – well she's not very experienced. I mean. What, is she fresh out of jail?

PAULA. Pretty much.

DAVID. Ralph was a great cutter. You couldn't have done any better?

PAULA. Bill wanted her in here

DAVID. Since when does that matter?

PAULA. Look... you know we've always hired ex-cons. Way back when, it was mob boys who got out and needed a job. And I've tried to do that too, to be – to be useful. But now...

DAVID. Now you're just doing it because it's all you can afford.

PAULA *turns away.*

So how bad *is* it? ...Come on. If there's one thing I know, it's money.

PAULA *sighs.*

PAULA. The insurance, the – the – *fucking* taxes, man, I... Brookshire raised the cost of almost all their beef cuts by two dollars a pound. I raised my prices in turn, you know what happened?

DAVID. Our beef sales were down last month.

PAULA *nods.*

Man I ground so many filets.

ACT ONE, SCENE TWO 29

PAULA. They're all going elsewhere. All the old families, y'know, they don't live here anymore.

DAVID. That's Williamsburg for you. They're priced out.

PAULA. Further and further every year, they'll be back in Sicily soon enough.

DAVID. So get on the frozen sausage train.

PAULA. I'm not gonna sink so low. My grandfather would roll over in his grave. And then he'd roll in here and slap me stupid. The store needs repairs, we could use refurbishing…

DAVID. So what do you need to do? Paula. I'm asking whose head's on the line.

PAULA. Not yours… I need a Junior Cutter with you, but I can't afford two.

DAVID. You mean…

PAULA. I think it's my only option. Ideal world, they both pass the cut test, I keep one of them, and give the other a good reference and send them to another store.

DAVID. Bill

PAULA. [Yes]. *One* of them. But yeah, JD's clearly the better cutter. And I've been paying Bill an apprentice salary for over a year now. I can't keep doing that if he fails again. Not if JD passes and becomes your junior.

DAVID. You think Bill would get hired anywhere else if he didn't pass?

PAULA. I can't say.

DAVID. He's improving… I've worked hard with him, you know that, right?

PAULA. I know, I know.

DAVID. He is trying.

PAULA. Sure, all of a sudden he's showing an interest. But it's too little too late. JD's hungry for it. He's got the goods to go all the way, you know?

DAVID *shrugs.*

DAVID. He's okay, sure

PAULA. He'll be a better cutter than both of us soon enough. T too, there's some serious potential there.

*A silence.* DAVID *shifts.*

What did you think?

DAVID. Yeah. Yeah she's alright… She's got cutter's hands for sure.

PAULA *smiles.*

PAULA. 'Cutter's hands.' You know I'm glad I took a chance on you, David. – Look, you're training Bill, do you wanna let him know about the situation?

DAVID. Sure. And JD?

PAULA. I'll talk to him. Alright. Go home. Get outta here.

DAVID. You coming?

PAULA. I gotta do some prep for tomorrow. See ya.

DAVID *waits a moment, but sees she's not going to budge. He exits.*

### Scene Three

*The following day.*

*The half pig carcass that was hanging from the meat hook is now flat on the central bench.* JD *helps* T *with trimming fat and removing bone, which they throw in a bucket. The bandsaw sounds intermittently from off as* DAVID *uses it.*

JD. Yeah, just leave a thin layer. Like bacon.

T. Bacon. Right.

JD. Oh, right. Uh. Just leave a little fat.

T. I'm a vegetarian, I don't live under a rock. I know what bacon looks like.

JD. Yeah. Of course. Sorry.
…Doesn't this gross you out?

T. Once the head is gone, not so much.

JD. So you said you learned how to cut… in… in jail?

T. Yeah I did this program, they taught us. Now it's just what I know how to do.

JD. You seem to like it though. You're good at it.

T *pauses.*

What

T. Nobody's ever said I'm good at anything before.

JD. Never…? I wonder if you'd be good at salsa.

T. No way man

JD. I'm gonna get you to dance, it's gonna happen… So like why don't you work at a… fruit store or something

T. Oh because vegetarians don't eat ice cream

JD. What?

T. Why would I work at a fruit store if I could work at an ice cream store

JD. Why *don't* you work at an ice cream store

T. I don't mind this. It's kind of… when I'm cutting it's… chill. Zen.

JD. Yeah. The meat's, like, your bitch

T. There are worse jobs in worse places. So I do it. For now. While I think about other stuff.

JD. What kind of other stuff?

T. Oh you know, settling down, getting married, moving to Wisconsin

JD. *Wisconsin*

T. *That's a joke*

JD. I thought that was, like… not a real place.

...

So you got someone to marry?

T. That was a joke too man, come on

JD. No I *know* I'm just

You know

*Wondering*

T (*teasing*). Oh, *wondering*

DAVID *enters with a tray of bones, breaking the moment.*

DAVID. That pig's not gonna salt itself, JD, let's go. I need you to clean the dry-age case after.

JD *groans.*

JD. Aw, you for real? Can T help?

DAVID. Like I'd put her through that.

JD (*to* T). It stinks in there

DAVID. It does. These, on the other hand.

*He takes a deep sniff of the bones.*

Nothin' like the smell of a fresh-cut femur. Get salting.

*He tosses an end piece at* JD, *who catches it and throws it in the trash.* DAVID *exits.*

JD. Fuckin Bernie. Paula asked him to do it but she's not in. – Just spread it all over like this, not too thick.

*He takes a container of seasoning and shows her how to rub it all over the carcass.*

T. What's his deal?

JD. What you mean

T. David. What's his deal? Why's he called Bernie

JD. Ohhh. So David used to be rich. Like real rich. Like he worked on Wall Street, had a car with a driver, stuff like that.

T. No!

JD. Yeah. But he was doing some mad shit with the money, like keeping it for himself. His house got searched by the feds and then it turned out he was snorting two grand of coke every week and his wife didn't know about any of it. And he went to jail and she divorced him and took his kids to California, and then he got out and became an alcoholic and then Paula took him in here and made a nice little cutter out of him.

T (*agape*). You're kidding

JD. Nope. Man grew up on Long Island, made it to FiDi, then fucked it right back to Queens. He got lucky – Paula has a habit of hiring people straight out of the pound. It's her thing. Except me.

T. Damn

JD. And we had another guy here, Ralph, you replaced him. He called David 'Bernie' after Bernie Mad– something, who had like, the biggest money fraud in history. Dave hates it.

T. Shit. Where's Ralph now

JD. He shot himself.

*Beat.*

So were you a vegetarian before…?

T. You're not gonna let this go

JD. I'm *curious!* You're a – a – what's the word – enema

T. …Enigma?

JD. Yeah. What's an enema then

T. …Google it. And no, I wasn't.

JD. But – but – what –

T. Alright. I learned to cut while I was inside. After I got out I got a job for Perdue in a chicken factory. I did everything, deboning, evisceration, marination… live hang, that's where you hang the chickens on the kill line. Upside down, by the legs, still squawking and flapping. You'd stop eating it too, if you saw that shit. This place is like a palace.

JD. Damn, really?

T. Then they moved me to Animal Welfare on a farm. Not much better. Spoiler alert, there is no welfare. Then I came here. Anything else?

JD. …No.

*A silence. They work.*

So, you have brothers or sisters?

T. You ask too many questions, man. No, I don't. Do you?

JD. I have two sisters.

T. You're the baby.

JD. How did you know!

T. You just seem like…

JD. A baby?

T. Not *a* baby. But like *the* baby, maybe.

JD. Maybe baby

…

Wait – sorry – I wasn't – I didn't mean to – like, to say baby to you

Like I – you're not baby – *my* baby – or *at all*

They just like, rhymed and… I don't know man.

Let's get her salted. Now this does need to be thick. Just get handfuls and – yeah, exactly.

*They rub mounds of salt on the carcass.*

You know after that wavy flat iron Paula will be your biggest fan.

T. She said it 'wasn't bad'.

JD. That's Paula. She's not gonna *show* you that she cares. She's like, cold. Bill calls her Frosty the Fuckin' Snowbitch.

*He laughs.* T *doesn't.*

T. Bill's… you don't have to copy what he does, you know? Like, you don't have to be a big man in front of me

JD. I'm – I – I'm not – I don't –

T. What about you, what brought you into this?

JD. Needed a job. It was this or sanitation

T. Right?!

JD. Yeah. And I like it. I wanna open up my own store some day.

T. Your own butcher shop?

JD. Yeah. You wanna work for me?

T. I'll work *with* you

JD. Oh yeah sorry, feminism or whatever

T. Feminism or whatever, yeah.

*Beat.*

Why's everyone call you 'dreamer'?

JD. Oh. Uh. It's – it doesn't matter.

T. You daydream a lot?

JD. No. Well. Yeah, actually. Head in the… clouds, or whatever. Alright, I'm gonna take this and do a wet cure –

T. Are you DACA?

JD. Huh?

T. Is that why they call you –

JD. Why you asking?

*T shrugs.*

T. Just... *wondering.*

*She smiles. He relaxes.*

JD. Uh. Yeah. I am.

T. Cool. Where you from?

JD. I'm Mexican. We came here when I was like two.

*T nods.*

What about you? Where you from?

*T is guarded, but he makes her laugh.*

T. I'm – whatever. I'm just from here. New York. That's it.

JD. Oooh, she's a *New Yorker.* Like you eat bagels 'n' lox and go to plays and shit?

T. No, like my bodega guy knows my order by heart and the people in my building are from Yemen, Tasmania and Cleveland and my grandmother died in a bedbug infestation.

JD. She *died*?!

T. *No.*

*They laugh. A silence.*

JD. ...Did you still wanna hang out later?

T. Yeah. I brought my glove. It's pretty beaten up but

JD. How beaten up? Is my hand gonna break catching your huge pitches?

*T retrieves a very battered looking baseball glove from her bag.*

JD. Shit. You need a new glove.

*He takes it.*

T. It's pretty old. It was my dad's.

JD. That's cool. What's his vibe?

T. Oh. I haven't seen him for… a long time.

JD. I'm sorry.

…

You know I bet I could fix this, like maybe re-lace it or something, patch the leather

T. For real? That – that would be great. Just – you know.

JD. I'll look after it, don't worry.

T. Yeah no I trust you

JD. You trust me? Big mistake man

*They laugh.*

DAVID *enters followed by* BILLY, *who goes over to the sausage-maker in the corner.* DAVID *carries a folder.*

DAVID. – Yeah if you wanna start on some sausages that'd be great, maybe something with chorizo – JD, man, if T's gonna distract you you can work separately

BILLY. Woah, Paula's little bitch got his panties in a wad

JD. Chill out Bernie, we're almost done

DAVID. Hey you don't talk to Paula like that so –

BILLY. What're you doing while we work?

DAVID. She asked me to check some stuff, I gotta go through the logs. T can you hop on the counter, be out front with customers?

T. Sure

JD. What you doing for Paula?

DAVID. I gotta look into those missing steaks, I said I'd do it today.

BILLY*'s ears prick up at this.*

JD. Huh?

DAVID. She didn't tell you? We haven't sold through sirloin for weeks and suddenly it's all been gone. There was so much left after the fourth

JD. Didn't we grind it?

DAVID. She thinks we got shorted on delivery. You know Paula. Very uh… meticulous, shall we say, meticulous.

JD. But I've checked all the deliveries –

BILLY. Yo dreamer, you want my sloppy seconds?

JD. NO

*BILLY scoops sausage meat out of the bottom of the machine and lobs it at JD. He ducks and it hits DAVID.*

BILLY. Shit!

DAVID. What the hell, Bill?!

BILLY. Sorry man, sorry, my fault

DAVID. Yeah no shit. Just get on with it, alright?

*DAVID exits, leaving his folder on a counter.*

T. *Sloppy seconds?* What is that

JD. It's all the sausage meat left at the bottom from the last batch

BILLY. Sausages, man, just pig shoved inside sheep. Here T look – mmm intestines. You wanna try it? OooOOOOoooo

*He pulls a trailing, dripping handful of white intestine from a bucket. He holds it close to her as she exits.*

T. No thanks.

JD. Nice work, man

*T exits, followed by JD. BILLY drops the act. He throws the intestine back in the bucket and goes over to David's folder. He opens it and looks through. DAVID enters with boxes on a trolley.*

BILLY. What's missing then

DAVID. That's what I gotta figure out. Some steaks, sirloin. Possibly some pork too. Can you grab the grind log?

BILLY. Probly just Paula being paranoid, no?

> DAVID *starts the process of comparing the boxes of meat with what's on the order forms in the folder.* BILLY *fetches the grind logbook.*

DAVID. I mean I didn't like to say it, but you know what she's like. And she's in pretty deep shit with money. If she doesn't find it she'll start doing pat-downs or something. Alright, untrimmed brisket… one, two –

BILLY. What you mean in deep shit? It's just a few steaks

DAVID. Yeah, it's a little more complicated than that… Paula's broke.

BILLY. Broke

DAVID. It's not just a few steaks. She's on thin ice. Losing money like a hemorrhaging fucking artery. And it's –

BILLY. You serious?

DAVID. Deadly serious. It's bad.

BILLY. How bad

DAVID. …Look I was gonna wait, tell you over a beer or whatever but…

Someone's out after summer.

BILLY. Out where?

DAVID. Out out… She can't keep both of you, man.

BILLY. What?

DAVID. By the sounds of it she can barely keep any of us… Sure there's a lull after Labor Day but I don't know what she thinks she's gonna do at Thanksgiving. Maybe she won't still be here –

BILLY. Wait wait. What you saying?

DAVID. She's got money for one of you to be my Junior.

BILLY. *One* of us?

DAVID. And she can't keep you on your Apprentice wage if you fail.

BILLY. Shit

DAVID. I'll push for you, man, but I can't take the test for you. You gotta pass, and you gotta show her you want it. You shoulda heard her. Dreamer's gonna come for my job next.

BILLY. Does he know? JD?

DAVID. I don't know. She's gonna talk to him… check the grind log for me, what'd we grind on the fifth?

BILLY. Uh… uh. Chuck eighty-five, twenty pounds; grass-fed ninety, ten pounds –

T *enters.*

T. Hey, I got a lady wants… this thing I've never heard of… Ass Boo Co??

DAVID. Osso buco. Sure – Bill just go through it against that list, okay?

T. Thanks.

T *and* DAVID *exit.*

BILLY *is highly stressed. He paces. Then he checks David's list and feverishly writes fake numbers into the grind log.* T *enters holding a pork tenderloin.*

You find the steaks?

BILLY. Uh. Yeah. Right here. We ground them, see.

T. You okay man?

BILLY. Yeah I – what're you doing with that?

T. Grinding it

BILLY. A pork tenderloin? Nah there's pork grinds out

T. The lady asked. It's for her dog.

BILLY. Her *dog?* Ground tenderloin for her – Jesus Christ

T. I know. It's a chihuahua.

*As she exits:*

BILLY. Yo T

T. Yeah

BILLY. ...I gotta talk to you about something

T. Lemme just do this

BILLY. Right now

T. What is it? I'm kinda busy

BILLY. You wanna help me with something

T. ...Sure

*Beat.*

BILLY. I took them. The steaks.

T *laughs and then realises he's serious.*

T. You... you what

BILLY. I sold it on already, there's no trail. I made three hundred bucks selling that shit. Now I got a guy in Kingsborough Houses wants grass-fed steaks for his kid.

T. But – but why would you –

BILLY. Because I need money, T. For my mom. I need it.

T. But – you can't just –

BILLY. Paula noticed the steaks, fine. But she didn't notice the grinds, or the sausage, or the lamb.

T (*incredulous*). What?! What've you been taking?!

BILLY. Paula sells one steak for more than what I earn in two hours. Or *this* bitch, who grinds a tenderloin?! That dog eats better than we do.

T. I can't believe you

BILLY. Shhh... I didn't have no choice, T, I need money. And now – now I guess I'm gonna lose this job!

T. What do you mean

BILLY. Dave told me. She's not keeping both me and JD. So I gotta up this, right now, and I need you.

T. Need me to what, steal meat?

BILLY. I'll tell you exactly what to take and when.

T. No!

BILLY. She figures it out, fine, you're just a temp, you're already gone, no proof of nothin'

T. You want me to take the heat for you? No, I'm not doing that

BILLY. Why?

T. You think I can risk going back inside? For petty theft? I just got out!

BILLY. *I'm* risking it!

T. That's your choice. How long've you been doing this? Since when?

BILLY. Since my mother needs treatment, and doctors, and hospitals. Since she can't work, and we can't make rent. Since I need insurance benefits, and money, fuckin money, for chemotherapy. I need you to help me. Please.

*A silence.*

T. I – I don't –

BILLY. Wow. You know the old T would have said yes, she would have said oh you need my help? Our family needs help? Anything. I'll do anything!

T. I will, but not that! I'm not going inside again. There's got to be some other –

BILLY. I been over the options, this is all I got. I need extra cash and I need it now. T. Please, come on –

T. I can't steal again, man, I – I can't.

*She makes to exit.*

BILLY. Then help me get the Junior job.

*She turns, waits.*

I'm not gonna get it over JD. Even if I pass. I know that.

T. Well. We'll get you a new job.

BILLY. With my record? Nah. I'm not gonna walk in to some other gig, T. And if I do, I don't have fuckin' ninety days to wait for insurance benefits to kick in. For me to move up, he needs to fail.

T. ...What are you –

BILLY. He'll have no problem getting something else. I need him out of the running.

T. You do it then!

BILLY. Paula will see right through that. No. You gotta –

T. I'm not doing nothing to JD, Bill

BILLY. Oh, I get it, you like him huh

T. No, I just

BILLY. C'mon, Juan Diego? The man so good his momma named him twice?

T. Bill, it's not –

BILLY. Aw. That's real cute, T.

T. Alright, we can figure something out, find some other way of making money, we could –

BILLY. Yeah. I found it. And I need you to help.

T. I'm not – I'm not doing that, I can't / be part of that stuff

BILLY. / You *won't*. Who took care of you? When your dad went inside? When you got out of juvie? Huh?

T.... Tía.

BILLY. Yeah. *My* mom. And now you get to pay her back. And you get to pay me back, for getting you this job. Which you fuckin begged me for, cuz you pussied out on the poultry factory and there's nothin else you can do. So cut the bullshit, T. You owe me, and you owe my mom. So you're gonna help us one way or another, yes? Yes?

DAVID *sticks his head in.*

DAVID. T, you done?

T. Sorry, one second

DAVID. Come on!

T *heads.*

BILLY. T? Yes?

T *stops, turns back to him.*

DAVID. Hurry it up, let's go

T (*to* BILL).... Yeah, okay.

T *exits.*

### Scene Four

*The following day, or in the ensuing days.*

T *and* PAULA *in the cut room.* PAULA *spatchcocks some chickens, leaving a pile of giblets.* T *works on tying a pork shoulder. She is agitated throughout, tries to hide it.*

JD *enters with a box, which he sets down on a workstation before opening it and completing an invoice form.*

JD. Man I hate that guy

PAULA. Who

JD. The wagyu delivery guy

PAULA. Oh. With the MAGA hat?

JD. Yeah. Every time! He looks at me like I'm about to rob him. It's like, bro, chill. You sell *foreign meat* for a living.

PAULA *laughs.*

What's this for, anyway?

PAULA. Customer order. Look at that thing. Beautiful.

JD. Maybe one day his Japanese cows will all turn against him. You should stop giving them your business Paula.

PAULA. He's Dave's buddy. Gets us a good price.

JD. *That's* a good price? This shit's *expensive*. 'Dave's buddy', come on –

PAULA *peers over T's shoulder and improves her technique.*

PAULA. Not bad. Tie it a little tighter though or it'll fall apart. Don't be afraid to show it who's boss.

PAULA *slaps the pork shoulder.*

JD. You know I bet Dave has a MAGA cap too. I bet he voted for him. Some of the shit he comes out with

PAULA. Well I wouldn't be surprised – given his background. But I'm not about to ask him.

JD. Well I do ask, and he's always like 'oh no I don't vote, just don't, never have' and I'm like well that's nice for you, Bernie

*The phone rings from off.* PAULA *heads to answer it.*

PAULA. Can you file that invoice and then do me some more skirt steak?

*He nods. As she exits:*

Nice job, T.

*A silence.* JD *senses something is up with* T. *He sharpens one of his knives and looks at the pile of giblets* PAULA *left.*

JD. You ever… you ever like, think about how the giblets in the chickens probably don't *belong* to that chicken…? Like they have loads of chickens and they take all the insides out to clean them up and then they just get shoved back inside any which way and so it's probably just full of other chickens' organs?

…T?

T. Huh?

JD. You good?

T. Yeah. Sorry. Just – focused on the pork butt

JD. Well focus on my porky butt for a sec. Also that's a pork shoulder

T. Right, sorry

JD. Alright I'ma put this away and stop distracting you

T. Alright, yeah, I'm almost done

*JD exits with the paperwork. T is alone. She checks the coast is clear and then goes to JD's knife set. She takes a sheet of sandpaper from her apron pocket, and feverishly dulls the knife against it. She checks over her shoulder. This continues until she's confident it's dull. She puts them away again as she hears voices off. She takes JD's cut glove from the bench and puts it in her pocket with the paper.*

*DAVID and BILLY enter and start getting their jackets and aprons on. JD follows them in. T gets back to work.*

BILLY. I mean, seventy? My abuela could do that, no cap

DAVID. Oh nice, is she single? I'd like to take her out

BILLY. You wanna go Dominican Republic and dig her up?

DAVID. Oh god!

BILLY. One fifteen to seventy, dogshit – sup T.

T. Hey

*PAULA enters.*

PAULA. Good afternoon, closers

DAVID. You sounded happy on the phone

PAULA. That was Donoghue's apologising for the mix-up, they can't see any error but they'll send a free box of thighs so. That's nice.

*A look between* T *and* BILLY, *very subtle.*

DAVID. As if they'd admit to any mistake on their part.

PAULA. Right. Anyway. Uh. Since I have you all here. I got something to say.

JD. Oop

PAULA. You've both been made aware through conversations with David and I that I only have one Junior Cutter position on offer at the end of summer. And I'm sorry. But you were all here on the fourth. You saw it. This business has been in my family for generations, and we've seen this neighbourhood through a lot. But it's changing, and unfortunately I gotta change too. So. I've been in contact with seven or eight butcher shops across Brooklyn and Queens, and three of them have space for a Cutter. No Apprentice roles.

BILLY *shifts.*

DAVID. None?

PAULA. Not right now. Some of the meat departments in the larger grocery stores also have vacancies – they have huge people turnover, always hiring. So there are options. Your cut tests are on Monday, and I want to see you both pass. Alright?

BILLY *and* JD *nod.* JD *stares at the ground.*

Guys I know this is shitty. But there's no point hiding it from you. Right, JD? If my cards are on the table, yours can be too.

JD. My – my *cards*

PAULA. I just mean you can have more time to figure out what's best. Don't fuckin panic, alright, I'm not just gonna throw you out on the street. It's not ideal but I want to help if I can. Okay?

BILLY. Yeah, thanks boss.

PAULA. Alright. Let's do it. I need some chicken sausage, Bill, and Dave, can you cut that wagyu?

DAVID. I was just about to prep that dry aged order

PAULA. Oh, shit, yeah. JD, can you handle the wagyu?

*T looks up in horror. JD nods.*

JD. Yeah

PAULA. You sure? I need some very thin steak cuts and then a quarter pound evenly cubed. With precision, alright? You confident with that?

JD. Yeah, of course

T. I – uh

PAULA. Great. Customer's coming in fifteen. Alright. Let's have a good day.

*PAULA exits. During the following, JD gets the wagyu ready on the counter. Then he looks around for his cut glove. T watches, unsure of what to do.*

JD. This sucks, man

BILLY. Yeah

DAVID. Don't worry about it, you'll be fine

BILLY. You're gonna pass

JD. Yeah, just sucks

BILLY. I know

JD. Where's my –

DAVID. What were we saying about your grandmother?

BILLY. Yo shut the hell up

DAVID, *laughing, exits.* BILLY *prepares the sausage maker.*

JD. You seen my glove?

T. …No.

JD *leaves the cut glove and just puts on latex gloves.*

Hey JD, don't – uh. Can I do it?

JD. Wagyu? No way, not – not yet

T. But I –

BILLY. T that shit is worth more than your left kidney – Alright I'ma grind this chicken

BILLY *exits.* T *hangs back.* JD *starts on the wagyu.* T *is so close to stopping him. He starts cutting and the knife goes sideways into the meat and catches at his finger. He gasps.*

JD. Ow! Shit

T. You okay?

JD. Yeah – shit

T. You cut yourself?

JD. It's fine, it's small.

*He checks his knife then looks at the steak.*

What the hell? – Oh man. Oh shit.

T. Maybe – maybe do the cubes with that piece

JD. It's too thin. Uh.

T. A different knife, maybe

*Flustered, he starts cubing the meat with a different knife.*

You know – I – maybe I can help?

JD. Nah it's fine

T. Check your knives –

JD. Leave it!

*Beat.*

T. JD. You're bleeding. You're bleeding *on* it. Look – just stop a sec. Go get a Band-Aid.

*JD reluctantly pulls away and exits. T throws the cut glove down and peers over at the steaks. BILLY enters to see what's happening.*

BILLY. What's going on? – Did he fuck it up?!

*T says nothing. BILLY picks up JD's knife. T turns away.*

It's not even – did you do this?

T. You said I had to do *something*

BILLY. Damn

T. He wasn't meant to be doing wagyu, I didn't –

BILLY. Nah this is perfect! Nice, T.

*PAULA enters, followed by JD. T backs away from the bench.*

PAULA. You better not have bled on an A5 wagyu

*She stops.*

What have you done to it?

*She picks up a couple of pieces.*

Are you kidding me? I can't sell this.

*She picks up his knife, checks the blade.*

Juan Diego, come on. Come on. What is this? Your first ever lesson, what was it?

JD. My – I –

PAULA. *SKOCH* [pronounced 'scotch'] – T, what is it?

JD. I know, I know what SKOCH is –

PAULA. Do you? Cuz you're acting like it's your first day. T what am I talking about? T?

T. ...SKOCH. Sharpen Knives Or / Cut Hands.

JD. / Cut Hands. I know

PAULA. I mean, look at these. That's your blood – where's your cut glove? And they're completely uneven, you've cut with the grain.

JD. I'm sorry, I –

PAULA. It's unsellable, I'm gonna have to re-order. You can explain to the customer why there's a delay.

*JD hangs his head and holds his cut hand.*

BILLY. Is it that bald guy? I took that order, I'll handle it.

PAULA. That's nice, Bill, but –

BILLY. He likes dry aged too. Maybe let's sell him some of that whisky-aged stuff

PAULA. ...Yeah. Okay. Can you –

BILLY. I'm on it boss

BILLY *exits.*

PAULA. JD. I know you were upset by what I just said about the job, but I can't have you making these kinds of mistakes right before your cut test.
...Here, show me

*She gestures for his hand.*

JD. You're not a doctor

PAULA. No but I can clean up a bloody animal when I see one.

*She inspects his hand.* BILLY *re-enters with a hunk of dry-aged beef.*

It's not too deep. Go get a Band-Aid, then take a fifteen, get a coffee or something. If I see you without your glove again...

JD *nods and exits in silence.*

BILLY. It's looking good. Let me sort something for what's left of this wagyu too boss

PAULA. Are you sure you can –

BILLY. Yeah, I got it. When your guy's here just come get me, I know him, we'll figure something out

PAULA. Alright then. Thanks Bill… Good job.

PAULA *exits.*

BILLY. *Nice.* That's what I'm talkin about, T.

*He holds out a hand to fist-bump. She doesn't.*

He's good, it's a tiny cut

T. He's humiliated!

BILLY. He's fine. She'll get over it. And that guy *is* my customer, and he owes me. He sold me shitty weed last week. Thank God, I'm gonna come out of this lookin' real good.

*JD enters, wrapping a Band-Aid around his finger. BILLY goes to him, claps him on the back.*

Don't worry about it bro, I got you. Shit happens to all of us, right? Sharpen your knives next time!

BILLY *exits.* JD *removes his apron and goes to get his bag.*

T. Are you okay?

JD. Fine.

T. It was just a mistake.

JD. Yeah well I can't afford mistakes right now, T.

*Beat. She is taken aback.*

How could I be so fuckin' dumb

T. Don't worry about it, it's okay –

JD. No! It's not okay! You don't get it. I need to pass this test, and I – if I can't –

T. You will pass! Of course you will

JD. You don't know Paula. If she thinks I'm not ready she won't even let me *take* it

T. You are / ready, JD

JD. / I can't fuck this up, I *can't*

*DAVID enters to get some trays from a cupboard.*

DAVID. Oof. Of all the things to fuck up it had to be a wagyu. You know you're not supposed to butcher your*self* right

JD (*mumbling*). Shut up, Dave

DAVID (*gently mocking*). Aw. Buddy.

JD. I said shut up!

*JD dabs at his face and turns away. T places a hand on JD's arm.*

DAVID. Yikes.

*He makes a face at T and exits.*

T. What's going on with you?

JD. I just need the job. That's all.

T. Yeah. But. I bet you could get a different one.

JD. No. I can't.

T. This isn't the only butchers in Brooklyn. I bet she'd get you into any of those places.

JD. It's not that simple.

T. Well. You're good. I'm – I'm sure you'll do great wherever you go.

JD. See. Even you don't think I'm good enough.

T. I do! Hey – I do

*She steps in front of him as he tries to walk away. At some point,* DAVID *appears in the doorway with an armful of trays. He sees them sharing a moment. He listens in, unseen, curious.*

I'm just saying that even if you didn't get *this* job, it wouldn't be the end of the world.

JD *doesn't respond.*

You know, I had to *beg* Bill to get me in here. And even then it's only temporary. Come on. She obviously wants to keep you… It's kinda lame how unconfident you are. That's not cool, man.

*She gets a laugh.*

You're never gonna get your own store if you're not confident. And that's a nice dream, dreamer. Don't get too down on it.

JD (*mumbling*). Never gonna get it anyway.

T. Huh?

*A brief silence while he considers.*

JD. …Can I… can I trust you with something?

T. Yeah

JD. I need this job because… Nah. Forget it

T. Go on

JD. Nah, nah

T. JD

*He pauses.*

What is it?

JD. …My DACA's up. It's up.

T. Oh. What does that mean?

JD. It means… You have to refresh it, to like, stay legal. It lasts two years at a time. And during that time you can work. But it expired.

T. So… you can't work?

JD. I shouldn't be.

## ACT ONE, SCENE FOUR 55

DAVID *backs up and leaves.*

T. Shit. When did it expire?

JD. Like two weeks ago. Our rent went up. My sister lost her job, I'm trying to help with groceries and stuff. I want to save and renew it, but…

T. Does Paula know?

JD. No! She'd probably have to fire me. She hasn't noticed yet. But that's the problem. I can't get another job without it. Nobody will hire me. They can't.

T. Shit.

JD. So… I can't mess this up. I can't afford to renew it on an Apprentice wage. And with everything going on out there… I need to renew it. I have to pass.

*T thinks, is silent.*

T, I haven't told *anyone*. It was killing me. Please, don't –

T. I won't, I won't. I promise.

DAVID *enters.*

DAVID. You on your break? We need some ribs when you're back

JD. Okay. I'm gonna take a fifteen. I have to do my assessment book.

DAVID. Sure thing, dreamer

*As* JD *leaves:*

T. Wait. Could I – could I help you? With the book?

*He smiles.*

JD. Sure.

*They both exit.* DAVID *turns to watch them leave.*

## Scene Five

*A couple of days later.*

*Music plays.* T, PAULA, BILLY *and* DAVID *work.*

DAVID. No but they need a fire in their assholes or they'll keep slobbing around and never win a title again, they need a star player to step up

BILLY. *What?* Like Aaron Judge ain't a star player?

DAVID. Sure he is but they're not getting it over the line, are they

BILLY. So the problem's managerial obviously

DAVID. Most problems are.

*He grins at* PAULA *as she gives him a long look.*

BILLY. That's real

DAVID. I FaceTimed my son the other day, first time in a while, you know what he was wearing? A fucking Ohtani jersey. I almost hung up.

*Laughter.*

(*To* T.) He's a player for the Dodgers

T. The Dodgers? I thought they were a professional dodgeball team

DAVID. No no, baseball

T. *Oh* cool

BILLY. She's fuckin' with you man

DAVID. Oh. That's right, I forgot you're a – a big fan.

T. The Yankees' problem isn't that there's no star player stepping up. It's self-sabotage. They're haunted by the success of Yankees past.

DAVID. Well, that's not –

T. And also they've been unlucky. Stanton's always injured, the team is totally unbalanced, plus their defence... absolutely stinks.

BILLY. Yooo call the fire department, she's hot as shit

DAVID. I mean, sure, that's one take –

BILLY. You're in the wrong field, T, should be a coach

PAULA. She's in the right field – don't be pushing out my woman cutters, now. We're on the verge of extinction.

BILLY. My bad, boss, my bad

PAULA. Yeah. We should be encouraging talent, Bill!

BILLY. Noted...

*BILLY exits with trays.*

PAULA. Yes. You do have talent. Before you ask.

T. ...I wasn't gonna ask.

PAULA. I thought your lamb racks were very neat this morning. And a customer commended your diced veal yesterday. Said it was very carefully done. So there you go.

DAVID. Diced veal's not talent, it's just cutting good cubes

PAULA. *We should be encouraging talent, Dave*

DAVID. Alright, alright, you're very gifted, T.

PAULA. That's better. T, just finish up those chicken thighs before you go.

*PAULA exits. DAVID sighs.*

DAVID. Typical Paula bullshit.

T. Where's the bullshit?

DAVID. Just...

(*He gestures after* PAULA.) Typical. That's all. Know what I mean?

*T doesn't respond.*

She wants to inspire you, because, you know, of course
she does. She'll always hire a girl if she can, and she'll do
anything to keep 'em. You're not supposed to say that, of
course.

BILLY *enters.*

BILLY. Schooling Bernie on any other sports?

DAVID. Very funny. I'll be out front.

DAVID *exits.*

T. God he's full of shit

BILLY. Aw nah he's alright. Imagine your kid moves to Cali
and becomes a Dodgers fan – Yo that was good yesterday.
You did it. Now we gotta think about what's next.

T. What's next? No I'm not doing anything else

BILLY. Yeah

T. No, man, no way

BILLY. I'm thinking we do this again before his test.

T. Are you for real?

BILLY. Once is a mistake, but twice, on the cut test –

T. That's fucked up

BILLY. ....Did you think this was it? This wasn't enough, T.

T. You saw him

BILLY. Yeah. I also saw my mom cough up blood this morning.

*Beat.*

We got these booklets due tomorrow, it's like a – an
assessment. Makes up twenty per cent of the cut test. I want
his answers.

T. I'm not doing –

BILLY. I'm not asking you to do something in front of his face,
or 'humiliate' him. I just need to copy his answers.

T *says nothing.*

## ACT ONE, SCENE FIVE 59

I haven't had time to study, T, I work as much OT as I can,
I go home, I do laundry, I make her food she doesn't want to
eat, I help her take a bath, I clean up –

T. I keep telling you to let me help –

BILLY. It's *my* mom, you don't need to help. You help by
helping me.

T. I can't – I can't do this to him, it's not right

BILLY. The hell's your problem, T? Huh?

T. I want you to get this job, Bill. I want her to get better!
I already give you half my paycheck. But I can't –

BILLY. Half your paycheck ain't shit, T. That's not enough.
Not compared with a Junior Cutter salary. And not compared
with the health insurance.

T. There's gotta be some other –

BILLY. Yeah. You refused.

*Beat.*

If you don't care, you can find some other place to stay. You
got enough for a deposit?

T. Oh, you – don't do that.

BILLY. She's always askin' where you at. You live with us but
you wouldn't know it.

T. I just got out of – I don't wanna sit inside all –

BILLY. She knows you don't give a shit

T. That's not true and you know it

BILLY. I'ma call her right now, let her know you gonna move
out. She'll be devastated, her only niece, her *preciosa
sobrina,* just wanted to live somewhere else

*He takes his phone out, starts to dial.*

T. Alright. Alright. Fine. I'll – tell me what to take.

BILLY. To take? Yeah?

T. I'm not gonna fuck with JD but I'll – I'll do this.

BILLY. Alright. Alright! It's gotta be when it's busy, so there's no way to point fingers, and focus on fresh stuff, not leftovers, she's less likely to miss it and I can get more money. I'll handle the deliveries.

T. But how much?

BILLY. Anything you can. Start small, now there's two of us.

T. Now? I'm about to leave.

*BILLY looks around. He takes an unopened pack of meat and gestures for her bag. She fetches her bag and he checks to make sure nobody's coming. She holds the bag open for him to put it in, but he holds the meat out to her instead, forcing her to secrete it herself.*

BILLY. Good. Now do that once every shift.

*She removes her apron and jacket.*

I'll get some porterhouse later, when Paula's gone. There'll be a delivery this afternoon.

T. And the job?

BILLY. I'ma do what I gotta do.

T. Bill.

BILLY. If you don't wanna know, don't ask. Selling this stuff will buy me some time and money if I don't pass the test.

*T nods, subdued, and turns away. DAVID enters.*

T. Thank you. Yeah?

*She doesn't look at him, but exits, taking her bag.*

DAVID. What was that about? She tell you?

BILLY. Tell me what

DAVID. Oh. No. Okay.

BILLY. What

DAVID. I just – I heard something the other day. I was gonna tell you… Later, after work. Just thought maybe she got there first.

BILLY. No, she's not been doing nothing for me, that's the problem. What is it…? What is it?

DAVID. Alright. Buckle up, Bill, this is juicy shit

BILLY. Oh yeah

*Beat.*

DAVID. Dreamer's not dreaming no more.

BILLY. What you mean

DAVID. You know what I mean.

BILLY. No *way*

DAVID. Uh huh

BILLY. Shit

DAVID. Yeah. So we go to Paula and he's out of here.

BILLY. My god.

DAVID. Yup

BILLY. You're serious?

DAVID. Yeah!

BILLY. Fuck! This is it, man! / This is it!

DAVID. / Yeah man, yeah. He can't work here. Seems like Paula didn't realise yet.

BILLY. Shit! Oh my god. Thank god, man, I – and… wait, and… T knows this?

DAVID. Yeah, I overheard him telling her. They were being all cute. He thought that wagyu was gonna be it for him, and –

BILLY. When was this?

DAVID. A couple days ago

BILLY. A *couple days* ago.

DAVID. Yeah. I was gonna tell you but you were off yesterday, with your mom – I didn't wanna –

BILLY *laughs.*

BILLY. *Puta de mierda.*

DAVID. Huh

BILLY. She – nothin. Nothin. A *couple days*?

DAVID. Sorry, man

BILLY. No no, no, not you. She just… that's it. That's it. Fuck, man.

DAVID. Well. You're welcome.

BILLY. Thank you, bro, thank you, thank you

*They fist bump or something similar. A moment of real joy.*

DAVID. You can breathe now, my friend. It's all you.

DAVID *exits.*

*Beat.*

*The smile falls from* BILLY*'s face. He leans on the counter. Relief, rage.*

## ACT TWO

### Scene One

*The following day.*

*Music, something upbeat. JD and T are side by side, him showing her some basic salsa steps. They perform them in unison. She's reluctant and awkward, but he's joyful. Then he turns away from her, takes two pig hooves and holds them in each hand under the sleeves, making it look like he has hoof-hands sticking out. He stands behind her and slowly reaches the hooves out on either side of her.*

T. Ohmygod NO – JD! Those are disgusting

JD (*squeaky voice*). Who me? Disgusting? I'm just a little piggy!

T (*laughing*). NO get away – NO I hate that

JD. Alright alright – here.

*He puts them down and turns down the music.*

That was so good though!

T. No, it was not

JD. It was! We gonna get a whole routine down

T. Thank god I'm only here a few more weeks

JD. Oh. Yeah. Man, that sucks.

*She smiles at him as his mood changes. Beat.*

I actually – I brought you – something

*He goes to his cubby and picks up a brown paper bag.*

T. I swear to god if there's a pig's head in there

JD (*acting crestfallen*). Oh. Oh... You don't want a pig head?

T. *NO* I – oh. Okay. What is it

JD. Close your eyes

T. I'm not doing that

JD. Close them

T. I'm not closing them

...

Alright fine

*She closes her eyes and opens her hands. He removes a wrapped gift but hesitates before giving it to her.*

...Should I open my eyes

JD. Just a sec

*He pauses, nervous.*

T. This better be good

*Too nervous, he puts the gift back and instead takes the trotters back up, and puts them into her outstretched hands. She opens her eyes and throws them down.*

NO ugh – oh god JD they're so creepy

JD (*squeaky piggy voice*). Come dance with me!

*He turns up the music and moves toward her, with the hoof-hands, dancing around.*

T. StOOOOp

PAULA *enters and stands there. They stop giggling and* JD *jumps to turn the speaker down, struggling with the hoof-hands situation.* T *does it for him.* PAULA *might normally make a snide yet good-humoured comment about getting to work, but she doesn't.*

JD. Alright – we'll leave that there.

T. Sorry, Paula – we only just –

PAULA *exits. They look at each other.*

JD. …Shit.

T. She's mad

JD. Yeah.

T. Maybe she had a shitty customer…?

JD. Maybe

T. Should we like, talk to her

JD. I mean… would you go near an angry dragon

T. What

JD. You don't – nah. When Paula's pissed – stay away from that shit. Should we go to Dunkin' after work? I want the little balls

T. You want the balls

JD. The balls. The holes. The / balls.

T. / The middle of the donuts? / Munchkins

JD. / Yeah munch – balls

DAVID *and* BILLY *enter and go to the jacket rack.*

Hey

BILLY (*yawning*). Afternoon, dreamer

JD. Tired much

BILLY. Yeah man

JD. Well wake up. She's ready for war today.

DAVID. Oh, good.

BILLY. What's up with her

PAULA *enters holding her phone which plays obnoxious hold music.*

PAULA. Afternoon team.

DAVID. How's it going

*She holds the phone up.* JD *boogies a little to the music.*

BILLY. What's that

PAULA. I'm on hold with a shipping company. Looking for my goddamn steaks. I was connected to them via a delivery service, who I was put through to by a New York state – farms – customer liaison line, who I got to via the accounting department at Pennsylvania Pork who I got to via their commercial customer service representative. So. It's going great, thanks.

DAVID. Fantastic.

PAULA. Can you cover the counter while I finish up? We can look at the beef set after. And Bill I need grinds. Pork and eighty-five to start with.

BILLY. Yes ma'am.

DAVID *exits.*

PAULA (*to* BILLY). I got your assessment book, by the way, thank you for that.

JD. Did you get mine??

PAULA. You put it into my hand on Monday.

*Beat.*

Yes, I have it.

JD. Thank God.

PAULA. You gonna stay late to make up the time you wasted messing around with those?

T *and* JD *turn to look at the trotters.*

JD. Uh

PAULA. Excellent.

BILLY. Knew dreamer had a pig kink

ACT TWO, SCENE ONE    67

JD. Ey don't say shit like that

*The hold music ends and a voice crackles through.*

PAULA. Yeah hello? One second – (*To* JD.) Clean the display windows, would you? And T, finish that chicken and then sink please – Yes hi, this is Paula Cafarelli…

PAULA *exits.*

JD. Ohhh man. My least favourite. And she knows it.

JD *retrieves some cleaning items from a cupboard.*

Alright smudges. Your boy's comin'.

JD *exits.*

*Beat.* BILLY *stares* T *down.*

T. You good?

BILLY. Do it.

T. Huh?

BILLY. Now. Do it.

T. Now? No, it's too/ busy

BILLY. / There won't be another chance today, do it

T. I'll / do it later

BILLY. / Now. All of those.

T. You said 'small amounts' – Bill –

BILLY *exits.* T *feverishly goes over to the tray rack and takes some pre-packed steaks, maybe three or four.*

*She goes to her bag and struggles to open it with the armful of steaks. Cursing, she kneels beside it, gets it open and starts to ram the packs inside.* JD *enters.* T *struggles to stand. He sees her right in the act.*

JD. Glass cleaner, glass clea–

*Beat.*

What – what're you doing

*She looks down at the steak in her hands.*

T. Uh. Nothing. It was just – I'm just gonna buy it.

*Beat.*

JD. …You usually have to buy it *before* you

*He gestures the bag.*

T. Yeah. Yeah I'm

I'm uh

I'm

JD. Vegetarian.

T. …It's for my aunt

*A silence. He steps slightly closer. Peers in the bag. She shrinks.*

JD. …*All* of that is for…

*He stares at her a while, cocks his head, making it make sense. Her mouth is like sawdust. She can't get words out. He backs away, shaking his head.*

T. It's not – JD

*He exits.*

*Fuck.* Fuck.

*She throws the steak in her hands to one side.*

BILLY *enters.*

He saw me. He fucking saw me

BILLY. Who

T. JD

BILLY. Aw, no

T. Why did you make me do it right now?

BILLY. Didn't *make* you do nothing

T. Bill

## ACT TWO, SCENE ONE 69

BILLY. I'll deal with JD

T. No, leave him alone, I'll fix it –

BILLY. Sure you will

T. ...I'm taking these out

BILLY. No. Leave it. It doesn't matter if you take them or leave them, he saw you anyway

T. He'll tell her!

BILLY *shrugs.*

Bill, please! What's your problem?

DAVID *enters with an armful of pork chops.*

DAVID. T can you cover me for a sec, I gotta butterfly ten thousand chops

T *looks to* BILLY. *He nods at her to go.*

T. ...Yeah.

T *exits.*

DAVID. Lazy son of a bitch slipped me a twenty

BILLY. Twenty bucks?! Gimme

DAVID. I didn't take it. I don't like working for tips, it's slimy.

BILLY. Alright Bernie, what a fuckin princess

DAVID *stops and faces him.*

DAVID. Don't be an asshole.

BILLY. ...Sorry man

DAVID. You good?

BILLY. She hasn't told me. She's not gonna tell me. She's really gonna keep his little secret and screw me.

DAVID. Shit, man.

BILLY. I don't know what to do.

DAVID. Tell Paula. About dreamer, tell her.

BILLY. I will. But T. What the hell, bro? She's supposed to be my family. I always looked out for her. When we was kids, I –

DAVID. She likes him. You know what they're like when they want some.

BILLY. Don't, man

DAVID. I'm just saying. You know how it is.

*DAVID collects his chops and exits, with a:*

Alright, six perfect pork chops for you, sir!

T *enters.*

T. I'm taking them out.

*She heads for her bag.* BILLY *follows, and doesn't let her get to the bag.*

BILLY. You hear her last night?

T. Tía? Coughing? Yeah.

BILLY. Not coughing. Choking. She's choking on her own blood that's in her own fuckin' lungs. I can't believe that's what you want for her. That that's how you want her to go out.

T. What are you *talking* about?!

BILLY. You made your choices. I think you'll regret it.

T. *What??*

PAULA *enters with* DAVID.

PAULA. Just while I have everyone and there's no customers – where's JD?

BILLY. Cleaning

PAULA. JD! Get in here!

DAVID. Uh oh

*He and* BILLY *share a snigger.*

ACT TWO, SCENE ONE 71

BILLY. Actually since he's not here, can I –

JD *enters.*

PAULA. You find the glass cleaner

JD. Uh. No.

PAULA *goes and digs it out of a cupboard.* JD *stares at the ground. As she does so:*

PAULA. Alright. All of you. Once again I am struggling to balance the books. I've made fourteen phone calls this morning, to suppliers, distributors, couriers. And the problem – the problem is the numbers add up. Until it gets here. Now, I think, I firmly believe, that we're just… making some errors somewhere. Too much red meat in the trim bucket, mis-labelling, maybe some of you are giving little discounts to your favourite customers…? But – and look I'm sorry, I don't – I don't *want* to do this, but I don't think I have a choice – until I find the answer there will be mandatory bag checks each time anyone leaves the store. I –

*Horror passes over* T*'s face.* DAVID *raises his eyebrows at* BILLY, *'told you so'.*

BILLY. You for real

PAULA. Yes. And again I don't *want*

BILLY. Then don't

PAULA. I understand that –

BILLY. You think because we did time that we're – that we're just – robbing you

PAULA. No. I don't.

BILLY. Then why you treating us like criminals?

PAULA. I'm not treating you like a criminal, Billy.

BILLY *is about to retaliate when* DAVID *touches his arm.*

And I'm not gonna have a fight with you about it. This is where I'm at right now. I'm sorry. Okay? I really am. I don't expect to find anything. And once the problem is solved,

I'll buy you a beer and you can yell at me and we'll move on. Alright? Let's go guys. Finish the glass, JD.

PAULA *exits.* T *and* JD *make eye contact across the room. Then he busies himself.*

BILLY. What the hell, can you believe her? The disrespect man, / the disrespect

DAVID. / I know – but you heard her, right, she doesn't know what else to do

BILLY. Don't take her side, bro

DAVID. No, no, I'm not. I don't want Paula looking through my shit either. But she's clutching at straws here

T *goes to* BILLY *but he ignores her and works on something. She waits for his attention, maybe tugs on his jacket.*

BILLY. It's not you she's looking at, man, I know Paula. Damn. It's like being back inside.

T. Bill

BILLY. Fuckin' – bunk checks and inspections – who does she think we are

T. Bill

DAVID. She's lost a lot of money, man, a *lot* of money – and yeah maybe we're not being careful enough but –

T. Bill

BILLY (*to* T). *What?*

*She is silent but looks at him imploringly.*

DAVID. Maybe start putting steaks down your pants instead, she won't search there

BILLY. Huh??

*He realises* DAVID *is joking and laughs.*

Yeah, yeah, I'd like to see her try

DAVID. Right?

ACT TWO, SCENE ONE   73

BILLY. Heyyy David just before you head out, can I just see real quick, just unzip your fly

DAVID. That's just my tri-tip

BILLY *laughs.*

See ya later Billy, oh wait what's that in your pants there

BILLY. What's that? That's just my pork loin, don't worry about it –

T. Bill, please –

BILLY. Goodnight Dave, mind if I just take a little peek down there, what's that

DAVID. Oh this? Nothing, just a rack of ribs, some oxtail and a kosher / chicken

BILLY. / A kosher fuckin chicken

*They both laugh.* JD *isn't looking at them.* T *hovers, terrified. She looks at the bag, starts to edge toward it.* BILLY *sees her.*

Yo T, I got some more dishes for you right here.

*He puts them into her hands.* PAULA *sticks her head in.*

PAULA (*to* DAVID). Counter – and display case. JD. I'm not asking again.

DAVID *follows* PAULA *out.*

*Beat.*

BILLY. She said uh, display case

JD *nods.*

JD. Yeah.

*He checks the time. He turns and faces* BILLY, T *caught between them.*

BILLY. So… are you gonna do it?

*Beat.*

JD. ... T?

T. Yes?

JD. Would you mind cleaning the glass for me?

*He holds out the bottle of glass cleaner.*

BILLY. Dreamer! You lazy son of a gun.

JD. Yeah.

T. I – I need to –

JD. Go ahead. Thanks.

*T pauses, then goes to him and takes it. She waits.*

BILLY. You don't need to do his dirty work, T.

JD. Go on.

*T pauses then exits. JD goes to her bag.*

BILLY. What you doing? Get out of there – Don't. Don't do that.

*JD looks up.*

JD. So you know, then.

BILLY. Know what

JD. What's in here

BILLY. I don't know.

*JD takes the steaks out.*

Put it back.

JD. She'll get in trouble!

BILLY. Put it the fuck back, JD.

*JD puts the bag back and puts the steaks on a cart shelf.*

JD. You don't care – ? Did you put her up to it?

BILLY. What you talking about

JD. Is this all on you?

## ACT TWO, SCENE ONE　　75

BILLY. What's your problem, huh? / What you doing?

JD. / Get off me

*Just as* BILLY *grabs at* JD *and they start to tussle,* PAULA *enters, followed by* T.

PAULA. JD, if I ask you – what are you doing?

BILLY. Nothin', nothin'

*They separate.* JD *whips his apron and jacket off and throws them in the basket.*

PAULA. Hey, if I ask you to do something, I expect *you* to do it, not for you to hand it over to someone else if you can't be bothered. What's gotten into you?

JD. Sorry about that.

PAULA. Alright. You two, your bags please.

*He takes his bag and opens it up.* PAULA *peers inside.*

Thank you.

JD. No problem.

PAULA. See how easy that is, Bill? Okay, T? You mind if I –

T *is slowly removing her apron and jacket.*

T. …Yeah. I mean – no, you can… yeah. Just – yeah.

PAULA *picks up the bag. Unzips it. Looks inside. Beat. She holds the bag out.*

PAULA. Thanks.

T. …Huh

PAULA. I'm just checking them, T, not keeping them. Here.

*T, dumbfounded, takes it, and looks inside. Then looks at* BILLY *in surprise.* BILLY *stares down* JD.

Once again, I'm sorry for making you do that, I appreciate your co-operation. Now go on home. I'll see you tomorrow.

T *stumbles towards the door, followed by* JD.

BILLY. You know JD's DACA is finished.

   T *looks at* BILLY.

   JD *looks at* T.

   T *looks at* JD, *shakes her head frantically.*

PAULA. What?

BILLY. JD? His DACA. Is expired.

PAULA (*to* JD). Is it??

JD. Thanks a lot, T.

   JD *tries to leave.*

T. I didn't! I didn't

PAULA. Woah there. Is it expired?

   JD *doesn't say anything.*

BILLY. It is, right

PAULA. I'm not asking you

BILLY. T told me

T. I didn't! I did not tell him, JD I swear

PAULA. Does everybody know about this?

JD. If you paid attention you'd know.

PAULA. Hey now

BILLY. Fighting words, man

T. How do you know, who told you

BILLY. Don't you remember, you did

T. I did not fucking tell you, who told you? – I swear, I didn't say anything

PAULA. JD when did it expire

JD. A couple weeks ago

PAULA. Shit.

BILLY. Yeah shit. So he's been here illegally /

PAULA. / Alright

BILLY. / And using you and your wages and –

PAULA. / Bill you can leave it

BILLY. / And, and he can't get the promotion, he can't, he can't move up and he can't stay here

T. Oh, my god, that is a shitty move Bill even from you

BILLY. Even from me? Even from me?? What you saying even from me

T. You really just out for yourself

BILLY. I'm just helping Paula out, I'm just giving her the information she needs to make her choices, she

T. You ran out of options huh

PAULA. That's enough. I would like to talk to JD alone. Your shift is finished, T, let's go.

BILLY. This affects all of us Paula

PAULA. If there isn't twenty pounds of eighty-five in that display case in ten minutes, your cut test can wait six more months.

*Beat.* PAULA's *dangerous when she's like this.*

BILLY (*grumbling*). The fuck, man

BILLY *exits, muttering. The grinder starts up.*

T. I didn't tell him, JD, I –

PAULA. Go on, T.

T. I didn't.

JD *nods, accepting this.*

JD. Okay.

T. Yeah?

*He nods. He believes her.*

PAULA. Thanks T.

T. …I'll wait outside.

*T exits.*

PAULA. Alright. You wanna tell me what the situation is here?

JD. It's expired, that's it

PAULA. Two weeks ago?

JD. Sixteen days.

PAULA. So what were you gonna do about that? Renew it?

JD. Of course! I just don't have the money right now… And you didn't say anything.

PAULA. Yeah. That's on me, I haven't been – there's been a lot going on

JD. So I thought if I could pass the cut test, move up, get the promotion, then I could afford it, and

PAULA. And you hoped I wouldn't notice until then.

*He nods.*

Shit. JD, I'm sorry.

*Beat.*

That must be very stressful. Is it?

JD. Just always looking over my shoulder, you know

PAULA. Yeah. Well. I can't – I can't promote you. If you can't work. You know that, right?

JD. I know

PAULA. You shouldn't be working at all.

JD. I know but I need this job, I –

PAULA. I know you do. I know.

JD. But you're gonna give it to Bill, right? I get it.

*A silence.*

PAULA. What do you need?

JD. What do you mean

PAULA. To renew it, what do you need?

JD. Money.

PAULA. How much

JD. I been saving what I can but I need a couple hundred more and I need to send the forms

PAULA. Okay. I gotta take you off my payroll

JD. No, please!

PAULA. Listen. I need you off my payroll. No paper trail, this could end me. You're on overnights until it's done. I can lend you what you need in cash. And I can give you a week to get it sent off. Can you do that?

*He stares at her.*

JD. I – I

PAULA. Can you do that?

JD. Yes. Yes.

PAULA. Alright. You come to the back door, eight p.m., I'll let you in. You don't come anywhere near here during opening hours until it's sorted. And when it is, you come back, do your cut test, – *pass* the fucking cut test – and I'll take what you owe me out of your paycheck. Got it?

JD. But – why

PAULA. Why do you wanna work here again?

JD. Uh. I – I like it.

PAULA. You like it?

JD. I love it.

PAULA. Yeah. You're passionate. And you're a talented cutter. I got some serious work to do to turn this shit around. I want you on my team.

JD. But Bill –

PAULA. Bill doesn't want it.

JD. Yeah he

PAULA. No. He's never wanted it. JD, he's never wanted it. I see it, I've had too many guys who are here because they don't know what else to do. This is that kind of job. But it's a life, it's a way of life. You have to love it. I do.

JD. I do too.

PAULA. Bill needs money, so do we all. That's not a reason for me to keep him.

*A silence.*

JD. About Bill.

PAULA. Yeah.

JD. You know you've been having… uh. Nah. Nothing.

…

Did you decide this already? Like. To pick me

PAULA. I expect you to pass. Bill I don't know. But if you both do, there's a clear choice. I'm not gonna let some immigration bureaucracy get in the way of hiring the Junior I wanna hire. So we good?

JD. We good. I don't know what to say.

PAULA. Say 'thanks boss, I'll clean the grinder every day for a year'.

JD. Thanks boss…

## ACT TWO, SCENE ONE    81

PAULA. I'll take that. Get outta here.

> JD *exits.* PAULA *exhales. She clears some things away, she can't be still.* T *enters.*

T. Thank you.

PAULA. For what

T. Helping him.

PAULA. Oh. You don't have to thank me.

T. Yeah but. That's – it's really…

PAULA. Well he's a good kid.

T. Yeah… I didn't tell Bill. I don't know how he knew but –

PAULA. That's not my concern.

> T *nods.*

> You guys get on pretty well.

T. …Yeah. I – he's – nice.

PAULA. I'm glad he's nice. I'm glad *one* of them is fuckin' nice.

T. Yeah.

> Well.

> Thanks.

> T *turns to go.*

PAULA. And what about you? What do you have lined up after this?

T. I… nothing. I gotta start looking I guess… Why

PAULA. I've been thinking.

T. …Okay

PAULA. I can't afford a team of four. Not with two Juniors or a Junior and an Apprentice full-time, anyway… But I really can't manage with a team of three. I could keep you, part-time, on your current wage – it'd have to be flexible, just for now, maybe a couple days a week. I know it's not much, and it might not work for you. But if you were willing to extend your contract, maybe through Thanksgiving... I know it's a long shot on my behalf. But I like what you bring to us here. And I think you're a better cutter than you think you are.

T *shuffles, unsure of what to say.*

You could have a future in this. If you wanted. So. It's on the table. Just think about it.

T *nods. She turns to go.*


**Scene Two**

*The next day.*

BILLY *works on chicken. There's a lot of silence and a lot of tension. Throughout,* BILLY *bubbles with incandescent rage.* DAVID *enters to start his shift and goes to the apron rack.*

DAVID. Afternoon.

*More silence.* DAVID *gets ready and goes over to* BILLY.

Hey man.

BILLY *nods.*

T *enters to start her shift.*

T. Hey

DAVID. Hi. You closing with me?

T. Yes I am.

DAVID. Excellent.

T *gets her apron on.* PAULA *enters.*

PAULA. Bill, when you're done with that I need liver. Dave –

DAVID. You need veal

PAULA. T's on veal.

DAVID. Oh

PAULA. Can you get some skirt steak out?

DAVID. Sure

PAULA. Thanks. Let's keep it moving, we're a man down.

T. Yes boss.

  PAULA *exits, and* T *exits.*

  *A silence.*

DAVID. You wanna play some pool tonight?

BILLY. Gotta take my mom to the doctor.

DAVID. Oh. Okay. It's been a minute.

BILLY. What do you want me to do, man?

DAVID. I – nothing.

BILLY. Is it weed you want? Cuz I don't have anything for you

DAVID. No, no, I just – I just wanted to play pool and hang out.

BILLY. Yeah well. I can't right now, Dave.

DAVID (*stung*). ...Alright. No problem.

  *A long silence.*

  T *enters with a side of veal that she starts to prep.*

  BILLY *exits.*

  DAVID *squints at* T.

  Did you get laid?

T. Excuse me?

DAVID. Oh. That's a no, then

T. Mind your business, Bernie.

DAVID *nods and smiles.*

DAVID. Alriiight. Good for you two.

T *just keeps working.*

You can usually tell when Juan Diego's got a date. He buys short ribs. Makes them short rib tacos… What'd he do for you, buy you a falafel?

T. No.

*A silence.*

DAVID. This is gonna be a long night, huh.

*No response.*

Wow.

…

That veal's *dark*.

*No response.*

You know why it's that colour…? People always think it's cuz the meat is 'better'. But it's not that. It's fear. See this animal knew she was gonna die. Imagine her eyes all wide and white and her skinny little legs trembling. Some people don't like to think about that. But see, she was panicking. Maybe the first shot missed the brain and she was still alive for a minute. Or maybe she was just a really smart little baby cow. Either way, her heart was pounding. Rushing blood all round her body. That's why the meat is that colour. Blood. *Terror*. Cuz she was *scared*… Cool, huh?

BILLY *enters.* DAVID *picks up his trays ready to take out.*

We need that liver out, if you wanna do it after that.

BILLY *nods.* DAVID *exits.* T *shakes her head – 'jackass'.*

*Behind* T, BILLY *cleaves the chicken. She tries not to jump with each loud thud. Otherwise, silence. He throws some of the chicken into trays, turns to her.*

## ACT TWO, SCENE TWO    85

BILLY. Where'd you go last night

*Silence.*

I asked you a question.

T. You *and* Dave, both so curious.

BILLY. Huh?

T. What's it to you?

BILLY. You stay at JD's? You should stay forever. In fact I'll take your keys now. Ain't no space for traitors in my house.

T. Traitors?

BILLY. Yeah. Yeah. You knew. You knew about him and you didn't tell me.

T. Because I knew what you'd do! And you did it. You went right to Paula.

BILLY. Give me your keys.

*He gestures for them. She doesn't give them to him.*

T. You offered me a place to stay because you said you wanted to see me make it. But it was never about me was it? You don't care about my future. You brought me in here to cover your ass and –

BILLY. Sure, maybe. So?

T. So I'm not just gonna let you fuck JD over –

BILLY. See how you like it here when he's gone.

T. He's not gonna be gone, is he. She didn't fire him.

BILLY. Not yet

T. She won't.

BILLY. Then I'll deal with him myself

T. Oh yeah? What're you gonna do?

PAULA *sticks her head in.*

PAULA. I need that veal asap. Bill can you give her a hand? Two pounds packed right away, and more in the case.

BILLY. Sure, I'll help.

*He takes up a knife.* PAULA *pauses. She knows something's wrong.*

PAULA. You good?

*Beat.*

T. Yeah.

PAULA *nods and exits.*

BILLY. Yeah. We good.

*He throws down the knife.*

You can cut it all, T. Since you're Paula's little dog.

*He pants at her, sticks his tongue out. She doesn't move.*

Hurry it up. Come on, cut it. Impress me.

T. You're not gonna do anything to JD.

*He raises his eyebrows, then turns away.* T *waits a moment but he says nothing. She then squeezes past him and goes into the cupboard under his workstation for trays. She piles stew meat into them.*

I'm not scared of you. Nor is JD. You want the job, go get it. But you'll have to get it honourably.

BILLY. Honourably. Big word. This shit ain't honourable. It's political.

T. Political?

BILLY. Yeah, it's political

T. In what way is –

BILLY. If I have to explain then don't worry

T. No, I wanna know what you mean. Come on.

## ACT TWO, SCENE TWO    87

DAVID *enters partway through to collect the veal, but slows as he hears them.*

BILLY. It's political because it's bullshit. Because it's rigged. Doesn't matter how long you been here, how popular you are with the customers, how fast you work. Paula will pick who Paula wants. She'll do her interviews, she'll sit all secretive in her office with Bernie bitchin' about us. And then one of you wins. See? Political.

T. Yeah, that is political. You show her what you got, she chooses. That's called democracy.

BILLY. Nah. Cuz that's not fair.

T. Who said it had to be fair? Who said anything about –

BILLY. You know how it went for me? After I got out I was cleaning toilets at the Barclays Center. Fuckin' disgusting. Came in here one day, straight up asked Paula for a job, she said yes. She said she was excited to see me move up. And then the two opportunities I had, she didn't give me. She failed me twice. She passed Jamal, piece of shit, and then Shaun, straight outta diapers and Disney Channel, over me. And then they quit anyway.

T. You ever think of asking? Why you didn't get it?

BILLY. I 'wasn't ready'. I'm ready. I been ready. I got customers that like me. I do overnights any time she asks. She said I gotta work on being a team player, work on my attitude. Bullshit. She likes fucking with me. She gets off on it. She says she likes giving people chances, so where's mine, huh? See she likes saving people, she likes saving guys who got nowhere else to go. It's all a big game to her, and I'm just a – a chess piece for her to play with. Right?

*He turns to* DAVID, *who shrugs.*

All honesty I don't care what Paula thinks. But it's her choice. I been here longer than dreamer boy. But she'll put us up against each other, and then she'll fail me. And if I walk, I don't get a job. She'll call up all her buddies and tell them not to hire me cuz I quit on her. She fuckin' hates a quitter, Paula. *'Winners never quit, quitters never win.'* And if I stay, I still don't pass the test. Because it's whatever Paula wants when she wants it.

T. Or it might be because you don't actually care? And she knows you don't care? And you don't try? You just *expect* –

BILLY. Nah, see. You don't know how –

T. Oh right I don't know how it goes. How many shots you got and all that. I know. Cuz you're actually really smart, right, Bill? But you flunked high school, whoops. But *you* didn't fail, right? The *system* failed *you*. Yeah. I guess nobody saw any potential in you.

DAVID. Ouch

T. So now there are, what, four options? One. You take a job making coffee for rich college kids, or stacking shelves of almond butter for their rich moms, or cleaning piss and beer off the floor at the Barclays Center. Check! Two, you find a trade, something skilled, something like this. Something you enjoy just enough that every day of the rest of your life doesn't feel like wading through mud. Check. Three, you try the Department of Sanitation. That application's a rite of passage, no? Spend your life picking up other people's trash, or shovelling snow off the sidewalk if you're lucky. That's Bill's back-up, Dave. Or maybe the MTA. If the background checks are lacking.

DAVID. Shit

BILLY. Fuck you.

T. Or option four, you fuck it all up. And you go to jail, like maybe your dad or your brother. Check.

BILLY. You know what happened to my dad wasn't –

T. Who said I was talking about yours? Who said *any* of that wasn't about me too? Cuz it is. It's me, and you, and everyone else who comes in this place. You say this is all for your mom, but it's not. You always think you got it the worst. Nobody else matters, except you.

BILLY. Welcome to the real wor–

T. That guy you beat to a pulp? Fuck him. Fuck his life. You need a job, better fuck everyone else over to get it. You think the world owes you something and it doesn't. Paula doesn't owe you shit. You don't inherit your chance, Bill, you *fucking earn it.* And I'm earning it. I take my shots, and JD takes his, and it's not our fault you keep missing yours.

BILLY. Whatever, you don't know what you're talking about –

T. Yeah, I do. Cuz you've always been the same. You will never make it in here. So yeah, in ten years, when you're still spending every Saturday night sitting on your mom's stoop alone, or with him – (*She indicates* DAVID.) smoking blunts in your huge sweaters that don't hide the fact that you're a fucking failure, I'm gonna look out my window and see you, freezing your snow-shrivelled balls off while you pick up my trash off the sidewalk. You've always been like this, big man, and you always will be. Your mom knows it too. You have always been a big fucking disappointment to her.

*A silence. They stare each other down.* BILLY *looks away first.* DAVID *reaches for the veal trays.*

DAVID. Can someone please cut some liver strips?

*He exits.*

BILLY. Real nice little speech. Did you practice that on JD when you finally took his dick out your mouth?

*T doesn't respond. She returns to the remaining veal and cuts.*

You – you're… fuck. Fuck me, man… That was low… You're nasty. You know? Nasty. On the inside. You're… shit, man.

BILLY *starts preparing liver on a fresh board. Liver is slimy, wet, and has the strong metallic odour of blood.*

*A long silence. Both are shaken up.* BILLY *throws the liver into trays.* T *needs more trays, but they're in the cupboard under* BILLY*'s workstation.*

T. I need a tray.

…

Bill.

*He ignores her. She goes over.*

Excuse me.

*He doesn't acknowledge.*

I need a tray.

*No response.*

Can I get into the cupboard? Bill. Can you please –

*At 'please', he steps slightly aside, continuing to cut liver. Not unaware of how vulnerable it feels, she crouches. His worktop is a big, bloody puddle. Then in one swift motion, he tilts the huge cutting board downwards, and sweeps the watery blood all over her head. It gets in her mouth, in her eyes, all over her.*

*A beat of silence.*

*Then she stands, making sounds of disgust.*

T. Urgh – oh my god – urgh

BILLY. Oops.

T. Why did you do that?!

BILLY. / I'm so sorry, oh man, I can't believe it, I'm so sorry T –

T. / You fucking asshole – you did that on purpose –

*Hearing commotion,* DAVID *enters. They all talk over each other.*

DAVID. What happened? What the fuck, Bill? Look at this

BILLY. It was an accident, I didn't –

T. It was not an accident, you poured it on me

BILLY. Of course it was an accident

T. That's BULLSHIT, it was not an accident!

ACT TWO, SCENE TWO 91

PAULA *enters.*

PAULA. What's going on, what happened?!

T. / He poured it on me –

BILLY. / I was just cleaning my boards and I accidentally got some on her / because I didn't realise she was –

T. / No, you tipped it over my head!

PAULA. Is that true?

BILLY. No!

T. Yes!

PAULA. Alright! Enough.

BILLY. But I –

PAULA. ENOUGH. I have customers out there. T, are you alright?

T. I'm fine.

PAULA. Okay. Get cleaned up, then go home.

T *nods.*

BILLY. Don't go home. You're not welcome.

PAULA (*to* T). You have somewhere to go?

T. Yeah.

PAULA. Okay. Stay off the shop floor – go get washed up first.

T *exits.*

PAULA *looks at* BILLY *and sighs.*

BILLY. I didn't do anything.

PAULA. Alright.

BILLY. Paula!

PAULA. Fine. Clean this mess up, then come to my office and we'll talk about it. Two minutes.

PAULA *exits.* BILLY, *shaking with rage, kicks the cupboard. He curses under his breath.*

DAVID. What happened?

BILLY *shakes his head.*

What did you do?

*During the following,* DAVID *fetches sponges and paper towels and starts cleaning up.*

BILLY. *I* didn't fuckin' – she just… it doesn't matter. It doesn't fuckin' matter. Cuz I told Paula, you know, I told her, and she didn't do shit. He's still here. And now this. She made me – T – she wants me to fuck up, same as Paula. But of course it's my fault, of course it is, who else could it be did anything wrong. I see Paula's eyes, like I'm a stupid little kid she has to deal with because nobody else wants him. I'm done. I'm done done. End of the fuckin' line for me, man. She won't get rid of him. I'm done.

DAVID *stands, calmly balls up the paper towels and throws them out.*

DAVID. My first boss said to me, 'You wanna win? You better wipe out the competition.'

BILLY. Yeah, I tried, I –

DAVID. Nine months later I was twenty-three, earning six figures, golfing in the Hamptons on Sundays and spending weeknights doing the most fucking beautiful crystal lines you've ever seen.

BILLY. …So

DAVID. So what are you gonna do?

BILLY. There's nothing else –

DAVID. Give me your phone.

BILLY. Why

DAVID. Just give it to me.

BILLY *hands his phone over.* DAVID *looks for something.*

BILLY. What are you doing?

...

Dave, man, what you doing

DAVID *hands back the phone.* BILLY *looks, and won't take it.*

What – nah. Nah bro, nah –

DAVID. Do you want the job or not?

BILLY. I – I can't –

DAVID. You said it. You're out of options. She's not giving you a good reference if you don't pass.

BILLY *hesitates.*

I want you to stay, man. So do it.

BILLY. Dave

DAVID. You wanna make your mom better?

DAVID *thrusts the phone toward him, but* BILLY *steps back.*

BILLY. No, man! No, I – no

PAULA *sticks her head in.*

PAULA. Bill. Come on.

*She exits.*

DAVID. Fine. Some people just don't know how to help themselves.

DAVID *presses dial, and lifts the phone to his ear.*

This is for you, man. You can thank me later. Go.

BILLY *exits.*

DAVID *waits while it rings.*

Yeah hello? Yes, I do.

*Blackout.*

## Scene Three

*Lights rise.*

*JD's overnight shift. Music plays. JD sharpens knives or cleans.*

*A knocking from off. He looks up, turns down the music and the knocking comes again. He exits.*

*JD and T's voices, off. Then both enter, T holding a coffee cup.*

JD. That's so sweet, you didn't have to –

T. I know, I thought you might be tired

JD. You did keep me up last night

T. Hey!

JD. I mean like, you kick a lot in your sleep

T. Oh okay that's what / you meant

JD. / Yeah, yeah

*Beat. He steps forward. She pulls away a little, maybe ducks around him gently.*

T (*quietly*). Feel like I still smell like blood

JD. Oh. I don't think so, I smell my shampoo

T. No I do, I smell like – like liver

*JD takes a strand of her hair and smells it.*

JD. No. You just smell like me.

*He tucks the strands behind her ear.*

You okay?

T. Yeah. – Here

JD. Thank you, that's so nice

*He takes the cup, sips it, makes a face.*

T. What?

ACT TWO, SCENE THREE    95

JD. God that's – oof

T. Oh yeah I couldn't remember how many sugars, so I just

*She takes a dozen sugar packets out of her pocket and dumps them on the counter.*

JD. Wow. Yeah I usually like six or seven

T. You're kidding me. I thought it was four!

JD. If we're being real, like… to be honest… I hate coffee.

T. JD you drink it every day

JD. Yeah cuz everyone else does, so. It's…

T. It's…?

JD. Like. Grown up.

*She nods.*

My first day Paula offered to buy a round. I wasn't gonna say 'no can I have a hot chocolate instead'. So I told her four sugars because that seemed… reasonable. And drinkable.

T *laughs.*

To be honest I snuck in some beers so I might stick with that

T. You have beer?

JD. Yeah. It's an overnight tradition! It's a long lonely night here without a couple beers. And what Paula doesn't know won't hurt her. Want one?

T. Sure, I guess

*He gets her a bottle.*

JD. That shirt looks nice on you.

*She looks down. It's one of his. Way too big. It has Godzilla or Tupac or something embarrassing.*

T. If you say so.

JD. I do. You can keep it if you want.

T. Oh wow. Thanks.

JD. So you don't know what happened with Bill?

T. No. I guess we'll find out.

JD. But she wants to keep you?

T. Well that's what she said. She also said she has no money.

JD. If Paula wants something she'll figure out a way to get it.

T. Like with you

JD. Exactly.

T. …I don't think it's gonna happen.

JD. What do you mean

T. I mean… I can't. I can't do it to Bill. And David's so… I don't know.

JD. What's David got to do with it? No. Don't let him get to you. You deserve this.

T. Bill's my family. For me to stay here if he loses his job… I'll find something else.

JD. Where?

   T *shrugs*.

T. Wisconsin

   *He half-smiles.*

JD. Wish *I* could

T. No you don't.

JD. No. I don't even know where Wisconsin is.

T. …Me neither.

JD. You should, you're the American here

T. Don't say that.

JD. You are. You're American. You're lucky.

   *Beat.*

   Where would you go?

ACT TWO, SCENE THREE   97

T. I don't know.

JD. An ice cream store?

T. Another butcher, I guess. Like I said, I can't do anything else.

JD. Nah. If Paula wants you, it's more than just that. You gotta love it.

T. Paula… and you. You made me feel like it was worth it. I wasn't supposed to stay. I guess I didn't know you were gonna be so… so

JD. So…?

T. Persistent.

JD. Oh – yeah

T. What

JD. Nothing

I just thought you were gonna say like

cute

T. Well

That – that too. You are.

*He grins at her. She sips the beer.*

Oh my god

JD. What

T. It's like – so strong

It's like *bread*

JD. It's an IPA, it's hoppy

T. *Hoppy?*

JD. You don't like it?

T. No… I don't know… maybe

*She sips it again.*

JD....Please stay. Think how great it would be. She wants you. I want you.

T *smiles.*

...Give me ten years, I'll hire you in my store.

T. I thought we were working together.

JD. Well we can't do that if you disappear.

T. I guess that's true. What are we gonna call it?

JD. Uh. JDT?

T. That sounds like an illness.

JD. Uh. Meat... Meat.

T. Meat.

JD. Kings.

T. ...Meat Kings?

JD. Yeah! The Meat Kings. Incorporated.

T. We're incorporated now

JD. Yeah incorporated. Of... of Brooklyn Heights!

T. Last I checked this is *not* Brooklyn Heights, man

JD. Yeah but it could be. We could open a fancy store in Brooklyn Heights, why not?

T. Can you imagine the rent??

JD. Oh my god, are you always like this? Have a dream, T! BROOKLYN HEIGHTS! THE MEAT KINGS! Come on! What's Paula say, huh? The American Dream, baby!

T. You're so cheesy

JD. Sure I am. You love it. You're gonna have to do so much more dancing with me / – so much – so much – how about right now

T. No / – no – no – !

*He turns the music up, pulls her into a salsa step. She's improved. He turns down the music.*

JD. YES, T, look at that

T. Alright alright – hey I gotta be back for the mid at ten

JD. Yeah you're right, you should go. You have the key?

T. Yeah.

JD. I'll try not to wake you.

T. I don't mind.

JD. No?

*Beat. They kiss, lingering a moment.*

T. Okay

JD. Okay

T. Night.

JD. Goodnight.

*He kisses her briefly again, then follows her off and lets her out.*

*He re-enters.*

*He turns the music up and continues cleaning the knives.*

*Lights shift to show passage of time.*

### Scene Four

JD *continues with tasks – cleaning, stacking tubs, date-checking items, filling in Health and Safety forms. It lasts a while.*

*A knocking on the door. He doesn't hear over the music.*

*The knocking comes again. He listens.*

*The knocking again, louder, more insistent.*

*He goes to exit, then the sound of glass smashing from off.*

*He stops in his tracks, frozen. He starts to back up.*

*Then:*

*An ICE raid.*

*It is terrifying.*

*We should feel the horror of it. It is loud, violent, disorientating.*

*Hands reach for* JD's *body like mouths at a carcass.*

*He tries to flee. He can't.*

*Blackout.*


## Scene Five

*The next morning. The light somehow starker, the space disrupted.*

PAULA *is on the phone, looking dishevelled.* DAVID *and* BILLY *stand, leaning on the benches, maybe mumbling to each other uncomfortably. Nobody is yet in uniform.*

PAULA. I can do that, that's fine. Yes. Do you need the – yes do you need the insurance papers too or – Okay. No they just called me this morning, I have no idea. Right. Okay, great. Thanks.

*She hangs up.*

DAVID. So

PAULA. I have a meeting with a lawyer at two. Until then I think –

DAVID. Should we go?

PAULA. Go? No – no we're gonna open as normal.

DAVID. You're not even meant to be in

PAULA. What time is it

DAVID. Seven-twenty

PAULA. Alright let's – let's focus on getting the key stuff out. Some steaks, some chicken – Bill maybe you could check the grinder, see if it's damaged? And I'll get some plyboard in the broken door, put a sign out.

DAVID. You're serious?

PAULA. Beef first, then pork. Let's do it.

DAVID. Alright.

*T enters. They all stop.*

PAULA. Oh. You're early

T. Yeah I was looking for JD... what happened??

PAULA. Looking for him

T. Yeah. He didn't come home.

*Beat.*

Why, where is he

*She looks between them all.*

Paula

PAULA. We... we were raided last night.

T. Raided

PAULA. ...ICE came here.

*T gasps.*

So, I don't know –

*T rounds on BILLY.*

T. *You.*

BILLY. What

T. You did this

BILLY. I dint do shit

T. What you said yesterday – about dealing with him!

BILLY. This is not on me, T, back off

> T *turns back to* PAULA.

T. Where is he

PAULA. I don't know. I –

> T *turns back to* BILLY.

T. Where is he? / What did you do?

BILLY. / I don't know – I didn't do nothing!

PAULA. Listen. I've been trying to call him, I don't know if he was actually here when they came or –

T. He was here. I saw him, I stopped by

PAULA. What time was that?

T. Uh… one, one-thirty?

PAULA. And he was here then

T. Yeah, he was fine. They didn't tell you?

PAULA. I got a message at six a.m. saying the business had been raided and with a number to call.

T. So call it

PAULA. There's been no answer.

> T *snorts.*

T. I knew I should have stayed.

> T *takes her phone out, calls* JD.

PAULA. It's not your fault, T… It's mine.

T (*to* BILLY). What did you say to them

> BILLY *just throws his arms up in exasperation. No answer,* T *hangs up.*

PAULA. Well T we – we don't know anyth–

T. Immigration Enforcement just happened to know that someone with an expired DACA would be here, overnight, last night?

*Beat.*

BILLY *shifts uncomfortably.* PAULA *looks at him. She understands something.*

BILLY. *I* don't know how they knew that

T. They got a tip-off, obviously.

BILLY. Yeah maybe they did, it could have been anyone, anyone who knows him.

T. Yeah. Because that's the thing about JD, he was really hated by everyone who ever met him, right?

BILLY. T, you can't pin this on me, I didn't do it

T. There were four people who knew JD was in trouble, and four people who knew he was on overnights. And one person who had a problem with him.

BILLY. Plenty of people / had a problem with him

T. / You wanted him out, Paula wouldn't do it, you had nothing left –

BILLY. How could you think I would do that, I did not call them!

T. I know you did!

PAULA. T, this isn't helping

T. Is doing nothing helping?

PAULA. I'm not doing nothing – I have a meeting with a lawyer, I'll keep calling the number, we'll figure it out.

T. There's nothing to figure out. He's gone. I know how this goes. They don't come back.

DAVID. Can you afford the lawyer?

PAULA. No. I can't. But I'll work something out.

DAVID. Look on the bright side, T. Now Bill gets the Junior job, he can help his mom out –

T. You can keep your one friend in the world

DAVID. I was gonna say I hear Paula's hoping to keep you around for a little longer, too.

BILLY. Exactly. It's all worked out.

T. All worked out? All worked out? I – I –

*She stutters.*

BILLY. He was no good for you, T.

*Beat.*

T. FUCK YOU.

FUCK.

YOU.

I know this was you, Bill, it's clear

BILLY. Jesus, I did not do it, and it doesn't – you know, it doesn't matter if you think I did, think whatever you want. Whatever happened, Paula's right. We gotta move on, get to work. I still got my cut test tomorrow, right boss?

T *laughs.*

T. You're paper-thin, man

BILLY. I didn't.

Do.

Nothing.

PAULA. Well. T's right. They must have had a tip-off.

BILLY. It wasn't me! How many times do I have to say it!?

PAULA*'s tone is dangerous.*

PAULA. No. I mean. Surely you couldn't, right…? Remind me, Bill. Your mom's [Dominican], yes? And your dad…?

BILLY. …Why

PAULA. Just curious

BILLY. Why are you asking

PAULA. Just answer the question

BILLY. Yeah she's [Dominican].

PAULA. And your dad?

BILLY. He's from New Jersey, he's [Irish] originally.

PAULA. Irish. Cool. So you're kind of… second-gen immigrant, then?

BILLY. What's your point.

PAULA. My point is that there's not gonna be a cut test. And there's not gonna be a job.

BILLY. What? But – but there's –

PAULA. See my ancestors built this place from the ground up, and now it's destroyed.

BILLY. It's not destroyed, it's just the window!

PAULA. Whoever called it in put all of us in jeopardy. The whole business. God knows how big the fine will be.

BILLY. / But you can't just –

DAVID. / But Paula –

PAULA. But my point, Bill, is that whatever happens there will be no job *for you*. What you did to T yesterday was enough, and

BILLY. I didn't –

PAULA. Or the fact that your answers on the assessment paper were almost word for word the same as JD's – even the wrong ones.

BILLY. I – I –

PAULA. I have given you so many chances, Bill, more than you deserved, and –

BILLY. No, I – I ain't gonna – you're trying to screw me, you're –

PAULA. – And you've let me down again and again.

BILLY. This is discrimination!

PAULA. Discrimination?

BILLY. You been out to get me since the beginning! And if you try and kick me out for something *I didn't do,* I'll sue you, I'll fucking finish you –

PAULA. JD was good. But more than that he was passionate. He dared to give a shit. To actually fucking *try*. And you couldn't handle that. So you went for the jugular, didn't you?

BILLY. I didn't call them, I –

PAULA. Didn't you?

BILLY. No!

PAULA. Really?

BILLY. No! I – it was Dave, alright! It was David who called them!

PAULA *turns to* DAVID.

PAULA. David?

BILLY. Tell her, man! Tell her!

*Beat.*

DAVID (*quietly*). I didn't call anyone.

BILLY. Yes you did, I – no. No. I am not taking the blame for this, he called them!

DAVID. Why would I do that?

BILLY. Dave man, what you – he called them, yesterday

DAVID. I certainly did not.

BILLY. Dave cut it out, you did! He did!

ACT TWO, SCENE FIVE 107

PAULA. Dave…

DAVID. No way, Paula. Look. Here.

*Beat. He holds out his phone.*

Check my phone. Check his.

BILLY. You – oh, you – fuck, Dave – he did, see he – he used my phone to call –

T *gasps.*

He did!

T. Oh my god

DAVID. No, Paula, I didn't.

PAULA. See? This store stands for everything you don't.

BILLY. Paula, I –

PAULA. Because we were *all* the new kids here at one point. You're Dominican, and Irish, David's – I think, Dutch, and Scottish, I'm Italian, JD's Mexican. There's another land in our blood, our hearts are half out the door in the countries our families left behind. And despite all that, despite who *you* are, you fucked him over in the worst way possible.

BILLY. No, *he* did

PAULA. So you are not welcome here again.

BILLY. I swear, Paula, I swear I didn't –

PAULA. No more second chances.

BILLY. Boss! Come on boss –

PAULA. You can stop calling me that. I'm not your boss anymore.

BILLY. Paula, I didn't! Paula!

*She heads for the exit but doesn't leave.* BILLY *gets close to* DAVID.

Why you do that to me, man? Huh? HUH?

DAVID *doesn't make eye contact.* PAULA *holds the door open.*

*Beat.* BILLY *steps back from* DAVID. *He looks around, defeated.*

I hope they do close you down. I hope they take it all away. Bitch.

*He exits, thrusting his store-issued cap at her. The bell jingles as he leaves the store.* T *sinks down the wall to the floor.*

*A silence.*

DAVID. So. Beef?

PAULA. Beef.

*DAVID gets an apron and exits.*

*A silence.*

I'm so sorry, T.

T *says nothing.* PAULA *goes around to her. They sit in the quiet.*

I know Bill's your cousin –

T. It doesn't matter.

*Silence.*

PAULA. Do you wanna go home?

T. I don't – I don't have anywhere to go.

PAULA *nods.*

PAULA. Do you wanna try your hand at the pork set today?

T. …

Sure.

PAULA. Okay.

PAULA *helps* T *up.*

I'm gonna get JD's things. Maybe you could give them to his parents?

T *nods. She puts on a jacket and apron, watching* PAULA.

*At some point,* T *exits.*

PAULA *goes over to the bag area. She opens* JD*'s cubby and removes the items in there. Headphones, papers, a cap, a cut glove, a sweater, candy. Two of the beers he had been drinking on his overnight – she looks at them with a knowing, suspicious confusion. She handles everything carefully, puts it in a store-branded paper bag.*

DAVID *enters to fetch some trays.*

PAULA *takes a brown paper bag from* JD*'s cubby. She peers into it. It is the gift* JD *was too nervous to give* T *before.*

Do you know what this is?

DAVID *looks over. He shakes his head, shrugs. He exits with his trays.* PAULA, *curious, opens it. It's* T*'s baseball glove, shiny, good as new. She looks at it briefly, then places the glove in the bag with the other items.*

*Everything cleared out, she leaves the bag on the counter and exits. We linger on the bag a moment. Then –*

*Blackout.*

*End of play.*

**A Nick Hern Book**

*The Meat Kings! (Inc.) of Brooklyn Heights* first published in Great Britain as a paperback original in 2025 by Nick Hern Books Limited, The Glasshouse, 49a Goldhawk Road, London W12 8QP, in association with Papatango Theatre Company and Park Theatre

*The Meat Kings! (Inc.) of Brooklyn Heights* copyright © 2025 Hannah Doran

Hannah Doran has asserted her right to be identified as the author of this work

Cover design by William Andrews

Designed and typeset by Nick Hern Books, London
Printed in Great Britain by Mimeo Ltd, Huntingdon, Cambridgeshire PE29 6XX

A CIP catalogue record for this book is available from the British Library

ISBN 978 1 83904 422 9

**CAUTION** All rights whatsoever in this play are strictly reserved. Requests to reproduce the text in whole or in part should be addressed to the publisher. This book may not be used, in whole or in part, for the development or training of artificial intelligence technologies or systems.

**Amateur Performing Rights** Applications for performance, including readings and excerpts, by amateurs in the English language throughout the world should be addressed to the Performing Rights Department, Nick Hern Books, The Glasshouse, 49a Goldhawk Road, London W12 8QP, *tel* +44 (0)20 8749 4953, *email* rights@nickhernbooks.co.uk, except as follows:

*Australia:* ORiGiN Theatrical, *email* enquiries@originmusic.com.au, *web* www.origintheatrical.com.au

*New Zealand:* Play Bureau, 20 Rua Street, Mangapapa, Gisborne, 4010, *tel* +64 21 258 3998, *email* info@playbureau.com

**Professional Performing Rights** Applications for performance by professionals in any medium and in any language throughout the world (including by amateur stock companies in the USA and Canada) should be addressed in the first instance to Nick Hern Books.

No performance of any kind may be given unless a licence has been obtained. Applications should be made before rehearsals begin. Publication of this play does not necessarily indicate its availability for amateur performance.

www.nickhernbooks.co.uk/environmental-policy

Nick Hern Books' authorised representative in the EU is
Easy Access System Europe – Mustamäe tee 50, 10621 Tallinn, Estonia
*email* gpsr.requests@easproject.com